Sporting Memories of a Yorkshire Aussie

Geoff Sleight

I dedicate this book to my family: my wife Peggy; my younger sister,
Margaret; my two sons, Paul and Jeremy; and my two grandsons,
Reuben and George.

I would like to thank my Editor, Claire Selishta, Quill and Scroll Editing. Claire has been professional, kind and meticulous throughout the whole process. Claire has also formatted and marketed the book. We have become firm friends during the time working together and without our chance encounter this book would never have been published. Claire's support and humour are very much appreciated.

INTRODUCTION

For many years, my wife has wanted me to write a book about my footballing life so that the future generations of our family will know all about my experiences. I never wanted to consider doing it until, in 2020, an Australian football journalist and historian called George Cotsanis wanted to interview me for a Melbourne radio station. Due to the coronavirus pandemic, this became a Zoom interview.

I asked him not to send me the questions beforehand. I said that I would just answer his enquiries off the top of my head at the time. About two minutes in, I realised that all he wanted to do initially was talk about how I had been coached. George is only in his early 50s, and in his experience, everybody is coached. Nowadays, there are more football coaches in Australia than there are kangaroos!

But I told him, "George, I didn't get coached."

"Well then, how did you learn to play?"

That inspired me to remember my experiences in those early years. George then posted our interview on YouTube. Following on from that, many other people started to tell me that I should write a book, in which I could expand on the stories I'd told in my interview. People would tell me that I've had a good life and I would reply, "I'm still having a good life!" Nevertheless, I decided to bite the bullet and tell my footballing story for my children, grandchildren and great-grandchildren etc... to come.

CHAPTER ONE

Early Years

Family Background

I don't think there's any particular significance in including my family tree or detailing my grandparents, but I will tell you a little about my parents.

My father's name was George Henry Sleight. We didn't have any sort of real relationship – my memory is of him bossing me around and telling me what to do at home. I was born on 20th June 1943; it was in the middle of the Second World War, and we had no money. My father was shot in the hand during the war. When he was in hospital, one of his fellow patients, a prisoner of war, was an artist. He drew sketches of myself and my mother from photographs which my mother sent him. They now hang in my home – the sketch of me is proof that at one time, I did have hair!

My father never took us on holiday anywhere, though my mother took us to Blackpool for four days in 1955, and for a week in 1956. By the time I was 16 years old, I was going off to Blackpool with the "lads" instead of with my family.

My father didn't support my footballing career much, although you might expect that he would have. I can only recall him watching me play football four times. I remember him once watching me play for Yorkshire Grammar Schools against Lincolnshire. That game ended 0–0 and I recall that he gave me a lift back home from where the match had been played in Cleethorpes. He then came to Manchester City when I made my first team debut on 16th September 1961. He came to Bolton the following Wednesday when we played against Fulham, and he came to Sunderland the following Monday when we played in the League Cup. That was it. He played football himself, but he didn't seem to be interested in my footballing life. His attendance at those matches didn't mean a lot to me, as I just didn't get on with him.

By contrast, my father clearly loved my younger sister, Margaret. She always got her own way and could twist him around her little finger. There is a four-and-a-half-year age difference between us. Margaret still lives nearby in Royston, and I go down most weekends to see her. She's very bossy with me and swears like a trooper — although she never swears if my wife Peggy comes with me. I think Margaret only really likes me for about six days a year. Peggy and I go on around four holidays a year to Barbados or somewhere warm and exotic, and I usually bring Margaret back 400 cigarettes each time. When I bring her those, she's nice to me for about a day and a half – then she goes back to normal! I treat her a lot more respectfully than she treats me!

My mother's maiden name was Edith Rowe. She was the one who showed support for me and my footballing career. Fortunately, she kept a lot of the early press cuttings about my games, starting at school level, and I have them now to refer to for this book.

School Football

It was at the age of seven that I moved up from the infant school to the junior school. I was old enough then to start playing football. I attended Royston Junior School, which was in the West Riding of Yorkshire. It was all boys, which probably made it easy to find a football team. I was the smallest one in the class at school, something I was well aware of as I was reminded about it often enough. It didn't bother me; my attitude was always, *I'll show them.* I think it made me more determined.

Growing up, I lived on a council estate in Royston. We used

gateposts as goals and played in the street – you didn't get cars driving around council estates back then. When playing football on the estate, you lived and died by your ability to stand up for yourself and survive. I was always the smallest in the group, and always the youngest. When I was seven, the other boys were eight, nine or even ten years old. If I hadn't learnt how to tackle, I would never have got a kick of the ball. My temperament was simply that I would not be pushed around, no matter how big the other lads were. I know people always say, "A good big one beats a good little one", but someone had to earn their money if they wanted to control me. It was necessary to learn how to tackle the big boys in order to get the ball, but from there, I then had to learn to dribble, because otherwise, they took the ball straight back off me and I was back to where I started.

Of equal value was the fact that all around the council estate, the gardens of the houses were separated from the road by a wall about two and a half feet tall. I think that must have been how the wall pass (the one-two) was invented – through boys like me practising up against walls like those. Also, the footpaths where people walked all had a kerb, so you learnt to chip the ball up over it. A quick wall pass, chip the ball over the kerb, and into the gatepost goal. That's a lot of football-learning without a coach in sight!

I went to Royston Junior School between 1950 and 1954. At

the age of 10, I played in the school team which won the league and the cup in 1954. In the old days, I played in the number eight position – inside-right – although there were no numbers on the shirts at that time. The old system was to have a goalkeeper, two full-backs, one centre-half, a right-half, a left-half, a right-winger, a left-winger, an inside-right, an inside-left and a centre-forward. Then, the Brazilians came along playing a 4–2–4 shape, and Alf Ramsey introduced the 4–3–3 formation when England won the World Cup in 1966. Now, it's all over the place: I don't know how you'd translate my original position of inside-right into today's terminology.

At the age of 11, I went on to Normanton Grammar School. As I made this transition, the bigger boys were all getting even larger, but I wasn't getting any bigger at all! I never got any taller than 5ft 4in, but in the grand scheme of things, it didn't really matter. If I'd been bigger and stronger, I would have been better, but even so, I would go on to play for England under-18 schoolboys.

When I played for the under-14s for the first time, I was 12 years old and in my second year at grammar school. I played for two years in that same inside-right position. To make it into the under-14s team at the age of 12, I had to be pretty talented, and I was. I could dribble the ball, I could tackle and, as I was getting older, I was getting quicker. I then went on to play in the under-15s team. By this time, I had been put on the

12

wing as I was smaller than the older players. I'm a right-footed player, but I played on the left wing. We didn't have a left-footed winger, and I could kick the ball better with my left foot than any of the other right-footers. Instead of going around the outside of a player and crossing the ball when I didn't want to, I could go up the inside and shoot. As I got older, this meant that I scored a lot of goals as well as creating them.

At the time when I was in the under-15s team, we had a very forward-looking headteacher. He organised a tour of Brighton and London for both the first 11 and the under-15s team during the February half term in 1957. I was 13, the youngest player in the under-15s, and the smallest player in the whole group. We played Hove Grammar School and Finchley Grammar School, then we went to Oxford and were taken to the theatre to watch *South Sea Bubble*. I fell asleep and got into trouble for wrapping my legs around the neck of the person sitting in the seat in front of me (who wasn't one of our party!).

On the Friday afternoon, we set off from Wakefield Station and I can remember us all being so excited to get on the train down to London. All of a sudden, my mother turned up to see me — what a nightmare! I tried to hide from her, but she saw me in the crowd and called out to me in front of all the other boys and the teachers. She said goodbye to me and gave me ten bob (50 pence). I forgave her quickly, because I used the

13

money to buy a combined trainspotting book – for which I got told off by the headteacher for "wasting money".

As a boy, I was a trainspotter. In those days it was a common hobby, usually passed down to you by older boys. You would buy a train book and then underline the names of various trains as you saw them. There were about 180 different trains in the Jubilee class alone. I first started becoming interested in trains when I was about eight or nine. I lived in Royston, and for the seven years when I went to grammar school in Normanton, I went on the train every day to travel the eight or nine miles between the two. On that journey, you would see the same trains all the time. To see different engines, I could go to Leeds, which was where other lines ran. There were four lines: LMS (London, Midland and Scottish), LNER (London North-Eastern), Western Railway and Southern Railway.

When we went to Blackpool on holiday in 1956, we went to Preston, which was another red-hot place for trainspotters. There, you could see engines that we didn't get coming into Leeds. I remember speaking to some lads from Preston and when I got really excited at seeing a particular train, they said, "Oh, it comes through here every day." When I replied that I took the train named *Repulse* regularly to go to school, they became equally excited and envious of me! If a train was common in your part of the country it would become boring to you, but to fellow trainspotters from another area where they never got to see that particular engine, it would be thrilling. Each engine had a little disc on the front that told you which shed it came from: Royston was 20D and Leeds was 20A. On my trip to London, I knew that I would get to see trains from the south and west that I'd never seen before, so it was very exciting. My interest faded away as I got older and more interested in girls, of course. Wine, women and song took over!

Anyway, during our school football trip, we beat Hove Grammar School 11–0. I scored the second goal. In the second match, we beat Finchley Grammar School 8–1. Again, I scored the second goal. Finchley's PE teacher was a man called George Robb, who had played for England when they lost 6–3 to Hungary in 1953. We were so pleased that we had beaten the team of somebody who had played for England. That match in 1953 was the first time a foreign side had beaten England at Wembley. The two main players in the Hungarian side were Ferenc Puskás and Nándor Hidegkuti, and they became household names. Hungary lost to West Germany in the World Cup Final of 1954, even though they had beaten the Germans 8–3 in one of the earlier group games. The following year, England played Hungary again, this time in Budapest, and were beaten 7–1. Ivor Broadis, who played for Manchester City, scored England's only goal.

While I was at Normanton Grammar School, I went for trials

with the Yorkshire Grammar Schools team. I wasn't that bothered about getting in — by this time, I was more interested in having girlfriends and I didn't really fancy the idea of having to travel to games at weekends and so on. But I had built up a reputation among the other grammar schools that I played against, so I was sent to have a trial. Afterwards, I was invited to go to Doncaster on Boxing Day 1960. The Yorkshire Grammar Schools team were playing Lancashire and I was added to the squad. I didn't want to go because it was Christmas — I wanted to go out with my friends and have a beer instead. However, my dad made me go. I took my girlfriend with me, and I remember that it was absolutely freezing. There were no substitutes in those days, and I didn't get to play. After the match, they told me, "Be at Halifax tomorrow, because we are playing Derbyshire, Nottinghamshire and Leicestershire and you're playing."

I played in the match the following day against the combined Derbyshire, Nottinghamshire and Leicestershire team. We won 2–0 and I scored a goal. Three or four days later, we played Lincolnshire in Leeds. As I had scored a goal in the last game, I was picked to play. This was at the expense of another lad, Gordon Welford, who was dropped. Gordon went to Barnsley Grammar School and had been a regular in the team up until then. I never saw him again. We beat Lincolnshire 6–2, and I scored four of the goals.

At this time, Yorkshire Grammar Schools had a really good team – a team which included Howard Wilkinson, who would go on to be a major figure in my career. That particular day in Leeds, I played almost directly against Graham Taylor, who was the captain of Lincolnshire. Graham later went on to manage Watford, Aston Villa, Wolves and England. 30-odd years later, when I was chief scout at Leeds United, Graham was the manager of Aston Villa. He came up to Elland Road to see Howard Wilkinson, who was managing Leeds. I went into his office and was introduced to Graham again. I told Howard that I recognised Graham from our schooldays.

"I remember you as well," Graham said. "Are you still as quick as you used to be?"

"No," I replied, "but I'm still quicker than you."

That was the last time I saw Graham; sadly, he died a few years ago. I know he was ridiculed by the media when he was England manager, but he was a gentleman.

I played six games for Yorkshire Grammar Schools that season, and in total scored seven goals. During the school holidays, when I was 16 years old, I played for the Barnsley Northern Intermediate team, which was an under-18s team. For most of the season I wasn't in the Barnsley team, just during the Christmas and Easter holidays. I must have been quite good, because whoever played in my position during the school term was always dropped when I became available to play in

17

the holidays.

England Boys

As the Yorkshire Grammar Schools side were such a good team, a lot of us were invited to the England schoolboy trials at Cambridge University in April 1961. There were 79 of us who went for four days, and what a magnificent four days we had. After the first day, the local newspaper actually reported as to which of us had done well so far in the trials. Things were being run by strong amateur people from the university, without professional experience. Before the start of the third day, they gathered us all together and said, "It's all going very well. We've had the first few trial games. But there's the odd person in the room here who possibly needs to learn how to pass the ball instead of dribbling it all the time."

They didn't mention any names, but everyone turned round and looked at me! I knew it was me they were talking about too, but I hadn't spent all that time on a council estate learning how to dribble only to pass the ball to somebody else!

Years later, in the 1990s, I went to visit all the Premier League clubs with Howard Wilkinson, when he was setting up the academy system. At Liverpool FC, we were talking to Steve Heighway — a flying right-footed left-winger, and another university guy. These academies were going to start coaching the kids at seven or eight years old. Howard said,

"I'll have to sit down and think carefully about how I would put a training session on for seven-year-old kids to teach them how to dribble and pass."

Steve replied, "Howard, you'll find that the best dribblers are the best passers. To dribble the ball, you've got to be able to control it, and if you can control it, then you can pass it." I've always remembered that comment because it justified my whole career.

The weather was fantastic the whole week we were in Cambridge. Every evening, we were out on the river on a punt, and then we would go to a pub called The Criterion. We weren't having six or seven pints; it was more like two or three. But we weren't supposed to go drinking, and if we'd been caught, we would've been sent home. I think I roomed with Howard Wilkinson that week. I was big into horseracing even then, and I remember making a little whip and sitting over the back of the settee to pretend that I was Lester Piggott riding in a horserace. I'm sure Howard would remember that too if I asked him, but he doesn't laugh and chat as much as I do. He does have a sense of humour, but it's very dry.

When it came to the final two games of the England schoolboy trials, those who were considered "probables" to be selected were going to play Corinthian Casuals, and those considered as "possibles" would play the England youth team. I was named in the "possibles" team – I think they were trying to make a point! They named a guy called Jim Bagby as left-winger in the "probables" team instead of me. The game against England youth was held, and afterwards, I didn't think I had played particularly well.

They then selected who would play against Scotland in an upcoming England under-18s match. They named 11 players and two travelling reserves just in case they were needed – their names were Roy Fitch and Alan Thompson. I had been playing in the number 11 position, so I had to wait while all the other names were read out for the 1 to 10 positions before finding out if I had been chosen. Eventually, they got to, "Number 11 – Geoff Sleight."

Yes! I had done it! Jim Bagby came up to me afterwards and offered his congratulations, even saying that he couldn't understand why they had picked him in the "probables" as he knew I was the better player. Looking back, my interpretation of it is that after they had indirectly told me I needed to pass the ball, putting me in the "possibles" was designed to really push that point home. I suspect that they were always going to pick me for the Scotland game because I was the best number 11, but they put Jim into the final trial game to give me a kick up the backside. It didn't work – I didn't change my game at all!

England schoolboys only played that one game against Scotland each year. We went up to Celtic Park to play Scotland the following week and lost 1–0 – a bit of a shock, because we were a very good team. We had John Jackson, who went on to play more than 300 games for Crystal Palace; Howard Wilkinson; Graham Taylor; Alec Brader and myself, all of whom went on to become professionals. There was only one guy from the Scotland team that I recognise now, and that's Andy Roxburgh. He went on to become the Scotland national team manager.

Figure 1 Royston Junior School team who won the League and the cup in 1954. I am on the front row, second from the left.

Figure 2 Normanton Grammar School under 14's football team. me sat at the front with the ball, the smallest by far.

Figure 3 Normanton Grammar School first XI cricket team in 1958. i am on the back row on the far right.

Figure 4 Normanton Grammar School first XI in 1960. i am on the back row, far left.

Figure 5 Relaxing with a 'beer' or two with Kevin Nixon on holiday in Blackpool, 1960.

Figure 6 Leaning on a clothes post in our unkept garden at Park View in Royston, 1960.

Figure 7 England Grammar Schools versus Scotland Grammar Schools, April 1961. I am on the front row, far right.

CHAPTER TWO

Bolton Wanderers

Trial and Reserve Team Matches

There was a scout who lived in Normanton called Harold Mason. He obviously knew about me as a schoolboy player, even though I didn't know about him. Every July, Bolton Wanderers held trials for schoolboys and amateur players. Harold Mason suggested to Bolton that they invite me for trial. I had arranged to work at Butlins Holiday Camp at Pwllheli to earn a bit of pocket money during the school summer holidays of 1961. Bolton wrote to my father and asked if I could go on trial with them, to which my response was, "So long as it doesn't interfere with me going to Butlins."

It didn't, as it was scheduled to be before I went to Pwllheli. Three of us from Normanton Grammar School went across one Friday afternoon. We played a full 11 against 11 match, and I didn't think I'd done particularly well. However, they must have been happy with what they saw, because a day later, they wrote to ask my father for his permission to send me to Bolton for a month during the school holidays. I agreed to go, and then wrote to Butlins to tell them, sending back the train ticket they had provided. I should have gone on 1st August, but back then, the bank holiday was the first Monday in August, not the last Monday. As a result, I instead went the week after, arriving on 8th August 1961, which was a key date in my development.

I was 18 years old and joining the first team and reserves for training. At this stage, I wasn't thinking about where my career might take me; I just took things in my stride. I never thought I had a future in the game – I just played each game and did what I could.

During that month, I was the subject of various reports in the *Bolton Evening News* and in *The Buff*, which was the Saturday sports paper. They said things such as, "Normanton Grammar School boy is the best wing prospect for years." They were assessing me as I went along. In the first week, they said things like, "Sleight turns out his tricks in practice." Other reports read:

Sleight Has The Right Idea

Geoffrey Sleight, a young Yorkshire amateur left-winger, fulfilled the promise of trial games when playing for Bolton Wanderers Reserves against Newcastle United in the Central League. He did all that could be expected from a youth making his Central League debut, showing speed, ball control, confidence, the ability to beat a man and passing effectively. Sleight started a move which resulted in Francis Lee scoring the only goal of the game.

Sleight Hits Winner For Reserves Against Preston North End

Another encouraging performance came from Geoff Sleight. His winning goal, two minutes from time, was a just reward.

Sleight "Shimmy!"

One of the personalities who believes Sleight is the goods is Nat Lofthouse. When Geoff scored against Preston, his little shimmy round a full-back "sent both me and George Hunt the wrong way as well," says Nat. Sitting there in the trainer's box, eyes glued on the ball at Sleight's feet, they both guessed the wrong way and so did the right-back.

Nat Lofthouse was known as "The Lion of Vienna" after he played with a broken arm in a 3–1 victory for England against Austria in Vienna. Nat had recently retired from playing and had just become assistant trainer at Burnden Park.

An amusing event concerning Nat occurred one day on the way to a reserves game at Aston Villa. We stopped for a pre-match lunch halfway through the journey. On the way back to the coach, Nat asked me to carry a bouquet of flowers that he had bought for his wife for their wedding anniversary. He felt embarrassed to carry the flowers himself – a true tough "lion!"

First Contract

I played my first match for the Bolton Reserves on 27th August. The team were playing twice a week at that stage, and I played six matches for them in all. Exactly four weeks after my time there had started, on 5th September 1961, I actually signed for Bolton Wanderers. It's quite an interesting story, because initially my intention had been to go part-time at Bolton while I also attended college in Manchester to become a PE teacher. The intention to become a teacher originated entirely from me, not from my parents. I had seven O Levels, including Maths and English, but left school before doing A Levels. There was no PE O Level back then, but if there had been, I would have had that as well. In those days, you didn't need A Levels to get into college. However, that didn't happen, because of what turned out to be my meteoric rise to fame, and I gave up the whole idea.

Bolton offered me a contract, and my dad took me over to sign it. It was for £20 a week. Prior to 1961, that was the maximum wage that any player could be paid — putting me in the company of Stanley Matthews, Nat Lofthouse, Tom Finney and all the most famous footballers of the time.

At around this time, the Professional Footballers' Association (PFA) were going to go to court against the Football Association (FA) to abolish the maximum wage. George

Eastham, who played for Arsenal, was going to be used as an example of the first player to be paid above the £20 limit. Any member of the PFA could've been used, but presumably George Eastham agreed for it to be him. I believe the FA were against the abolition because it represented progress, and they were in favour of the status quo. At the last minute, the FA withdrew – the PFA union, which was led by Jimmy Hill, won the case. Immediately, Johnny Haynes of Fulham and England became the first £100-a-week footballer, the highest-paid player in the UK and possibly the world. So, then I was on 20% of the highest-paid player! If you fast forward to the time of writing, Gareth Bale is reputedly being paid £600,000 a week at the moment. If I was on 20% of that, I would have been getting £125,000 a week, at 18 years old! I've often thought of writing to Bolton Wanderers for my "back pay"!

The "progress" that the FA were originally against has turned out to be a promotion of greed, in my view. For comparison, miners who were doing five shifts a week on a 2ft-high coal face were being paid roughly £20 a week, and miners who were the same age as me were only on about £4.50 a week, whereas I was going straight onto £20 a week. It would lead to too much wine, women and song.

As I walked out of the manager's office, having just signed my first contract, Alan Ball's dad was there. Alan was playing at Bolton then, and I knew him. His dad wished me congratulations, and I thanked him. I then asked why he was waiting to see the manager and he replied, "I'm going to get Alan's release. I'm taking him to Blackpool. Bolton were going to sign him, but they've signed you instead." My claim to fame is that Bolton signed me instead of Alan Ball! Just five years later, Alan played in the World Cup Final of 1966. If Geoff Hurst hadn't scored three goals that day, Alan would have been the man of the match. Perhaps Alan's claim to fame was that he knew me – but probably not!

During my trial period at Bolton Wanderers, I was in accommodation at 9 Ainslie Road, Bolton, being looked after by Mr and Mrs Pearl, who regularly took in Wanderers players. When I signed professionally with the club, I started to share digs at Mr and Mrs Pearl's house with Les Jones, a fellow Wanderers player. After Les left Bolton, I shared with Wyn Davies, Arthur Marsh and Jimmy Davidson. I settled in well to the digs, which was like a home away from home. At £4 per week full board, it cost considerably less than it would do nowadays, 60 years on! I think living with a married couple and being surrounded by other players meant that I didn't have a chance to think about missing home. I was focused on getting on with my life.

Soon after I signed my contract with Bolton, another article appeared in the local press:

Bolton Promotes Boy Sleight

32

Geoffrey Sleight, with one A-team match, six in the Central League and two weeks as a professional, starts on the dizzy trail to soccer stardom tomorrow when he steps out as Bolton Wanderers' outside left against Manchester City at Maine Road. A cruel casualty of injuries at Burnden Park gives the 18-year-old his chance so quickly, but I like the way the boy took the news. Manager Bill Ridding called Sleight into the office and said, "You're getting your chance, son." "Thank you, Sir," Sleight said, and walked out on the wings of wonderment.

I can't remember the manager calling me in! As I recall, I found out I was playing when we were on the bus going down to Burnden. We bought a *Daily Mirror* in which it said, "Young Winger To Make Debut For Wanderers." I wondered who it was and then realised, *Oh, it's me*! That same evening, I was walking across town to get the bus back to my digs. I remember seeing the newspaper placards showing that headline and the feeling of knowing that they were talking about me.

When I reached my digs, I was met by a freelance reporter and photographer, who took me back to Burnden Park to take pictures of me shooting at an archery target. The following morning, the photograph appeared in the *Daily Herald, Daily Express* and *Daily Mail* under the title of "The Bullseye Debut Boy" or "Lower Your Sights, Young Geoff". The photograph even appeared sometime later in a kids' comic called the *Tiger* along with such characters as Roy of the Rovers, Jet Ace Logan and Olac the Gladiator.

First Team Matches

My first team debut for Bolton Wanderers against Manchester City was on 16th September 1961. I originally made it into the team because Brian Pilkington, the regular left-winger, was injured. What surprised me most was that after lunch at the Pack Horse Hotel in Bolton, as the team coach departed for Maine Road, each player was given a packet of 20 Players No.3 cigarettes. Most footballers smoked in those days. Billy Bremner, of Leeds United, later died of cancer, and he in particular was a heavy smoker. I find it remarkable that cigarettes are still available at all. I think the main reason that they are is that governments are a bit hypocritical about it. They want to stop people smoking for health reasons, but they do it by putting more and more tax on cigarettes, so they still get their income from that, even though they're simultaneously telling people to stop smoking.

During my debut match, I didn't feel any pressure – I just treated it like any other game. To quote the newspaper headline from that Saturday evening:

Wanderers Go Down Fighting, Sleight Puts on a Show

Wanderers put up a brave fight at Manchester, but they could not quite equal City's clever raiding. Sleight, making his first team debut, showed up well, with some neat touches. Sleight made a beautiful move when he held the ball against two tackles before whipping it over the defenders' heads for Stevens running in. Sleight had a cheer to himself when he went back to help his colleagues and finish with a back pass to Hopkinson the goalkeeper. The Wanderers' best reply was a Birch run and cross which beat the goalkeeper Trautmann. Sleight returned the ball hard and low and it was cleared by the alert Cliff Sear near the line. Sleight did some clever probing as the Wanderers fought back against a Manchester side still inclined to over-kick the ball badly. The Wanderers were not done with them yet, and their frequent attacks found Sleight as good as anybody in the lead-up play, with skilful ball control. Sleight was hurt in a late tackle by Betts, but he quickly recovered and continued to do well.

On 20th September, I played against Fulham. For the first 20 minutes, I had a good time against George Cohen, who later became England's World Cup-winning full-back. We were on top in the early stages and had a lot of the ball. I can't remember much more about the game apart from Alan

Mullery scoring the winner in the 89th minute – Fulham won 3–2. Mullery also later became an established player in the England team.

It's so strange how we tend not to appreciate what might happen in the future. Now, 60 years after the night I played against Fulham, it turns out that the interviewer involved in helping me write this book is a dyed-in-the-wool Fulham supporter. Is this an example of every silver lining having a cloud? No, not at all. Without Michael Matthews' involvement, this book might never have been what it is.

Back in 1961, on 25th September, I played in a League Cup game against Sunderland. This was my third and final first team appearance for Bolton Wanderers. We lost 0–1 and Brian Clough scored the goal. Brian went on to manage Derby County and to lead Nottingham Forest to win the European Cup twice. Cloughy was brilliant as a manager; he didn't follow the traditional way of coaches and managers. He did things his 1 so different to everyone else. He was manager of Leeds United too, for 46 days. He followed Don Revie, who was an extremely successful manager. It was almost impossible for Clough to follow him. Players like Billy Bremner, Jack Charlton and Johnny Giles were at their peak, and Clough went in with his own style of man-management. As soon as Brian arrived, he took down everything related to Leeds' successes of the 1960s and 1970s which was up on the walls. It all caused a total clash, hence why he was only in the job 46 days. Funnily enough, I wasn't a big fan of Leeds in those days, even though I ended up as their chief scout years later.

It had been a month and a half since I'd gone on trial to Bolton instead of going to Butlins, but after three first team appearances, I was out. I played well enough in my first game to be picked again in my second game, and I played well enough against Fulham to be picked again for the Sunderland match. Then, however, Brian Pilkington came back from injury. I spent the next 18 months mainly in the reserves, playing occasionally in the A-team, which was the team below the reserves.

The reserve team played in the Central League – that was my level. It was a very good league, which they don't have nowadays – they have under-23s instead. In those days, they didn't have squads. You played in the first team or the reserve team, and there were no substitutes. If a player was dropped from the first team, or if they had been injured and were playing back to fitness, they would go into the reserves. I even remember Noel Cantwell (the captain of Ireland and a Manchester United full-back) playing against us in a reserve team, for example. There's none of that now.

Towards the end of that first season, we played Blackburn Rovers Reserves in the Lancashire Senior Cup on a Thursday night. I didn't think I played that badly, and I scored, but we lost 4–1. The following morning, I was called into the manager's office and got a rollicking for being "useless". I was told, "You would be down in the A-team on Saturday, but they've got a chance of winning the league, and with you in the team, they'd probably lose, so you're staying in the reserves."

Whether he was winding me up or not I don't know, but it worked. We went out against Blackburn Rovers again two days later, and I played better – I scored the first goal and we beat them 2–1. In some ways, you could say that the manager was very good psychologically, but he didn't *explain* why he thought I was playing badly.

Bolton had signed me because I could dribble the ball and pass it. However, when you're playing not so well and you run with the ball, it gets taken off you. You start by going past three or four players successfully. Then next time, you go past two men and then someone takes the ball off you. By the next time, the opposition are getting used to you, so they tackle you sooner and you don't get past anyone at all. The only thing I got told was not to dribble the ball – but that was why they'd signed me!

You'll also often get threatened by a big, silly full-back saying that if you go past him again, he'll break your leg. You try to take no notice, but you are aware of it. Sometimes, when you're feeling good, you'll give it a go and go past him anyway, but on a bad day you won't, because you're scared to death that they'll take the ball off you. That's where coaching comes in — but as I said, they didn't coach in those days. I lost my confidence to an extent, and I can't recall anything the club did back then to build my confidence back up. There was never any praise; you were more likely to get a rollicking, which would send your confidence further down.

Thankfully, things have changed since then. It's so different now, and it'll be even more different in another 10 or 20 years, because the game's changing so much. We've now got VAR (Video Assistant Referee) and whoever thought that would happen?

Fall from Fame

When my first season came to an end in April 1962, little did I realise that the forthcoming events over the next two and a half months would prove to be the beginning of the end of my career at Bolton Wanderers.

At the end of the season, I weighed 10 stone. When I returned for pre-season training towards the end of July, I weighed 11 stone and eight pounds. This was the result of a daily diet of steak, chips, cheese and too many pints of beer. There was no end-of-season training, which was the norm in those days, and that absence of physical activity was set against a backdrop of overeating, drinking and going horseracing every day. I'd assumed that pre-season training on my return to Bolton would get me back to fitness, but I didn't realise just how difficult this was going to be. Obviously, the club were not very happy with my appearance, and my performance in training was a nightmare, to say the least. With hindsight, I should have been placed on a weight loss diet and an appropriate fitness programme to get me back to my original weight of 10 stone. In the event, I only got down to 11 stone. Maybe I was stronger, but I certainly wasn't as effective without the pace that I'd lost.

I started the 1962/63 season in the Central League team, scoring after five minutes in the first game, a 3–1 victory over Sheffield Wednesday Reserves at Burnden Park. Howard Wilkinson played in this game, for the opposing team. After that, the only time I thought I had a chance of playing in the first team again was after I played at Old Trafford against Manchester United Reserves in October. I thought I'd done OK and might get picked for the first team once more, but obviously the manager disagreed with me. When the teams were put up on the Friday I was put in the A-team.

As the season progressed, I was in and out of the reserve team and the A-team, now vying for a place against younger up-and-coming players such as Gordon Taylor and Dennis Butler. The season was badly affected by the freezing and snowy weather, interrupting play for six weeks across December and January. I actually completed the season back in the reserve team.

The season finished at the end of April, but player contracts ran until June. In late April 1963, I read in the *Bolton Evening News* that Geoff Sleight and Dick Oxtoby were being released. That was the first and only time I received that news. I went home, and that was it. I was out of a job, although I continued to be paid until June. I had been with Bolton less than two years. A meteoric rise and a meteoric fall.

Had I thought that I would get back into the first team at some point? Yes and no. The usual process for a player would be that as you get older, you get better, and eventually make it into the first team. For me, I got into the first team when I was only just turning professional, so the expectations were very high. Every silver lining has a cloud – you could say that I peaked too soon, and there was only one way to go. I'm being wise after the event now, which is easy, but at the time, looking forwards was not nearly so easy. I always say, "If we knew what was going to happen in future, we'd all be down at the bookies!"

Figure 8 The 'bulls eye' debut boy, taken on the 15th
September 1961. Photograph appeared in the Tiger, a kids'
comic during the 1961/62 season.

Figure 9 Part of the team photograph for Bolton Wonderers, 1962

Figure 10 Bolton Wonderers Reserves programme, 24th March 1962

44

CHAPTER THREE

Leaving Bolton Wanderers

My Bolton contract ran out on 30th June 1963. I could've signed for a couple of other league clubs – Gillingham and Oldham come to mind. However, the pay at the lower league clubs would have been less. I considered getting a job and playing part-time. Then I was approached by Wigan Athletic, who were a non-league team in those days, playing in the Cheshire League. The Cheshire League was accepted as the best and strongest non-league division in the country. I signed for Wigan as a part-time professional in early July 1963, on pay of £11.50 per week plus a win bonus. That was reasonable money for non-league, but to get up to the £20 which I was used to having, I needed a job. I applied for and secured a job in the accounts section of the Bolton Corporation Transport Department. The post paid £8 per week. When I added that to my football wages at Wigan, I was getting £19.50 weekly, near enough to what I'd been getting at Bolton. I worked full-time in the accounts department, trained on Tuesday and Thursday evenings with Wigan, and played on Saturdays. It was different, but interesting. I asked Mrs Pearl if I could carry on living at 9 Ainslie Road, and she agreed.

Apart from scoring two headers against Wrexham in a 3–1 away victory, my time at Wigan is dominated by the memory of being sent off at Ellesmere Port. The referee reported that I had sworn at him, and that was the reason for him sending me off. That was simply not true. I swore at him *after* he sent me off! I admit that I'd deliberately kicked the full-back, and I was caught kicking him, right under the referee's nose. I had no problem with being sent off for that. However, for the referee to turn around and tell a lie was totally not on. I was suspended for three weeks.

However, those three weeks happily coincided with my wedding to my first wife, Lesley. I had met Lesley when I first started playing for Bolton Wanderers Reserves, towards the end of August 1961. She and three of her friends, Dorothy, Kathleen and Eleanor, supported the Wanderers and attended those early reserve team games. They thought that I must be lonely living away from home and wrote to me. I guess they were what would now be called groupies, and Lesley drew the short straw!

Lesley and I got married in Horwich Parish Church near Bolton, on 30th November 1963. I was 20 years old and she was 19. I remember that I had a very rowdy, heavy-drinking stag night at the Gardeners Arms in Bolton on 28th November. It was attended by all the Bolton Wanderers players. We'd decided not to have the stag do the night before the actual wedding, so that I wouldn't feel that bad on the day. Is it a coincidence that two days later, as I was getting married, Bolton were losing 0–

5 at Chelsea? Did they still have hangovers? My friends all got as drunk as I did during the stag do, and while I then turned up to my wedding without a headache, they went to Chelsea and lost heavily!

A spanner was thrown in the works shortly after signing for Wigan Athletic, when I received an approach from a team in Australia, Sydney Football Club Prague. They wrote to me on 24th July 1963, two weeks after I'd signed a one-season contract with Wigan. The first line of the letter read, "I have taken your name and address from the Professional Football Association transfer list for 1963." In other words, the PFA (the union) had distributed the names of available players all over the world, and that's how they'd found out about me. I think they reviewed the list each year, picked out a few players and wrote to them speculatively.

Sydney FC Prague was based in Australia, but it had been founded by a group of Czech Jews who defected from Czechoslovakia to Australia in the late 1950s. That happened quite a bit in those days and created a boom in Australian football. The teams, such as Prague, were often named in relation to where the owners originally came from, and they signed players from all over the world. For example, in addition to Prague there was Hakoah, who were also Jewish; Pan Hellenic, who were Greek; Apia, who were Italian; Polonia, who were Polish; and Melita Eagles, who were Maltese. There were also some Australian teams, like Cumberland, Canterbury and South Coast United.

I believe that the owners of Prague were so successful in business that they made enough money to run the club as a "hobby". Unfortunately, they began breaking the rules and signing players from other countries who weren't eligible to sign for them, because they were already committed to teams in their own countries. As a result, Australia were actually suspended from world football for five years by FIFA in 1959.

In their initial letter to me, money wasn't mentioned, so I wrote back to them and asked various questions. As I had expressed an interest in their approach, they then sent me a contract. They offered me a £100 signing-on fee (even though they said they didn't offer signing fees) and offered to pay my air fare to go out there. Sport, even including rugby league, was all part-time professional in Australia at that time, so I would need a daily job on top of my football, but they said they would get me a job paying £20 per week. They also said that they would get my wife, Lesley, a job paying £12–£15 per week. I didn't know what my job would be – I had to wait to find that out when I arrived – but they knew that I was clerically capable and had been informed of my O Level qualifications.

The contract also offered me £10 for every match I played, plus £5 if we lost, £10 if we drew and £20 if we won. If we won a match, I would get £30, plus my £20 wages for that week, plus my wife's £12 wages. On a top week, we could be bringing in £62.

I was 20 years old, and now thought I knew everything there was to know in the world because I'd moved out of home in Royston and lived in Bolton for two years. Looking back, I realise now that I knew nothing, or at least very little. Nevertheless, I could see that going to Australia would greatly expand my life experience and earning potential, so I agreed to their offer.

Prague wanted me to go through the migration process and apply to the Australian government to emigrate to the country. That process only cost £10 in those days (we were known as £10 poms), which was what they meant in the contract by saying that they'd pay for my air fare. By doing it this way, I knew I would have to stay for a minimum of two years. If I left Australia sooner than that, I would have to reimburse the government for the full cost of my outgoing air fare. I started the application process in around August or September 1963, and it could take anything up to a year, but the owners of the club were pushing for it to go through as quickly as possible. Ideally, they wanted me out there for the start of pre-season training in January 1964.

I was going there to replace a player called Alick Jeffrey, more or less arriving off the plane in Australia just as Alick boarded another plane back to the UK. The contrast between myself and Alick was stark, as he was a big lad, about 6ft 1in and around 14 stone. Alick had been a boy wonder, a real talent akin to Duncan Edwards, who in my opinion is the best footballer there's ever been. Duncan tragically died 14 days after the Munich air crash, from injuries he had sustained. Alick Jeffrey had actually been just about to sign for Manchester United when he unfortunately broke his leg very badly in two places while playing for England under-23s in 1957, when he was just 17 years old. The injury looked to have brought his career to an end, although he did recover and then went to Australia, where he played for Prague. Of course, if Alick hadn't broken his leg and had signed for Man Utd, he could easily have been in the Munich air disaster, so in a strange way, it was a lucky escape.

The next step was brilliant – Prague wrote to Wigan to tell them I was going to Australia and to ask for my release, but at that point, I hadn't mentioned anything about it to Wigan! I was hauled up in front of the board, where I acted a bit green and said I didn't know what the procedures were. I confirmed to them that my plan was to emigrate. I was formally released by Wigan in February 1964, but I continued playing for Wigan, and working for the Bolton Corporation, right until I left for Australia.

As the emigration application progressed, Lesley and I moved in with her parents, until we left for Australia. On 15th February 1964, I received an eight-day notice and telephone call to say that I was booked on a flight on 23rd February.

Figure 11 Programme, Wigan Athletic versus Buxton, 16th November 1963.

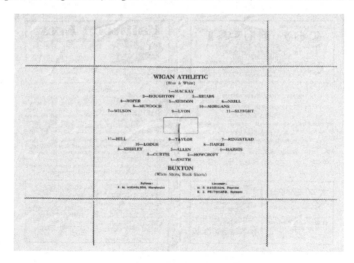

Figure 12 Inside the programme, Wigan Athletic versus Buxton teams.

Figure 13 Manchester City Reserves versus Bolton Wanders Reserves, 23rd October 1961.

CHAPTER FOUR

Australia

Going to Australia was a massive decision, and it seemed even more massive when we arrived at the end of our 30-odd-hour plane journey. It had been my first ever time on a plane. Nowadays, when you fly to Australia, you go from Manchester or London straight to Dubai, and then on from there to Sydney. When we went out there, we stopped for a minimum of two hours to refuel the plane at Frankfurt, Rome, Beirut, Tehran, New Delhi, Singapore, Darwin and then eventually got to Sydney. Our flight was on a Boeing 707, which was one of the leading planes of the time, but it didn't have anything like the fuel capacity that planes do today.

I had started off the journey feeling a bit strange. My mother and my sister, Margaret, came down to London for our last evening in the UK. Next morning, Lesley and I said goodbye to them and got on the bus at Victoria to go out to Heathrow. We were halfway to Heathrow, both feeling quite upset about what we were doing, when I looked out the window only to see my mother and sister in a taxi alongside us! They'd decided to come to the airport and stay with us for another few hours until we got on the plane.

Looking back now, I realise that there have been two or three big decisions I've taken that have been really key to my life.

Emigrating to Australia was definitely one of them. I didn't have a clue what Australia was like as I'd never been there – I didn't have the imagination or experience at that age that I have now, and any excitement was soon overtaken by apprehension.

When we arrived, we were met by the club and went to dinner with one of the owners, Sbinak Hoffer, and his family. They were lovely people, but we were so tired that we had to leave early. We were taken to a bedsit that the club had found for us at short notice in a place called Marrickville, an inner suburb of Sydney. We went to bed totally jetlagged. We then woke up the following morning, a Monday, to a rude awakening – we were 19 and 20 years old respectively, newly married, 10,000 miles from home, and we didn't know anybody in Australia. We both cried. Lesley was overwhelmed with a feeling of, *What am I doing here?* I had some experience of having moved away from home, although that was only from Royston to Bolton, so it was hardly comparable! When Lesley started crying, that upset me too. At one point that morning, I even said, "That's it, we're going back."

However, there was a stubbornness in my personality, along with a bit of ego, that wouldn't let me contemplate failure. Something inside me was very determined and knew that there was no way I was going back. I had committed for three seasons, and that's how long I was staying for, no matter what it was like. There was no way I was going to have people laughing at me for having made the journey, only to bottle it and come straight back. I would have done anything rather than lose face. I had strength, which meant I would fight the world if I had to. That stubborn streak had been there right from my childhood back on the council estate, when the bigger boys wouldn't let me have a kick of the ball. It's not something that you can call on — it calls on you, it directs you, and it would help me through a lot of problems during my time in Australia. I knew we would make a success of our situation there, and I remember thinking that we would show the world what we were capable of.

There were a couple of things that happened early on which really opened my eyes, showing me that I was a bit green and not as smart as I thought I was. The first of these was that the £62 I thought we would be earning wasn't actually £62 at all. An Australian pound was only worth 16 shillings against an English pound. That meant that instead of £62 in a good week, it was more like £50. However, £50 was still a long way above the £20 I'd been getting at Bolton. The second thing was that I discovered the Australians only played about 25 matches in a season that lasted six months. I had been playing about 50 matches in a nine-month season in the UK. I learnt the hard way, but I was young, and learning from mistakes is often the best way.

Another problem was that we'd only been there a week when we got burgled. They took my wife's engagement ring, wedding ring and camera. I knew who did it – he was the son of the owner of the apartments we were living in. If I saw him now, I'd sort him out. We should've been living somewhere posh like Bondi, but instead, we were in Marrickville, which was a Greek suburb. That's where we lived the entire time we were in Australia. In those days the migrants, or "new Australians", were the English, Greeks and Italians, and we were called "poms" or "wogs". In fact, a player called John Warren wrote a book called *Sheilas, Wogs and Poofters,* meaning women, migrants and homosexuals. Football players were often called "poofters" in Australia at that time. They had Aussie-rules football, rugby league and rugby union in the country, and by comparison, soccer players were considered soft. Even now, although football in Australia is improving, it's still a secondary sport in the country. All the kids play football, but it's not made that big step forward to become as big as cricket, Aussie-rules football or rugby.

As I've mentioned, the offer from the club had said that they would get me a job paying £20 per week or would pay me £20 per week until they found me a job. For the first week, I was given time to settle in and start going to training. Then, they got me a temporary job with a company owned by one of the club's directors that sold cardigans and jumpers. My role was looking at orders that came in, packing up the goods, and sending them out to the customer. I was working alongside one other guy and the boss. After a week or two, they got me an interview at a brewery, but the job only paid £17.50 per week, so I refused it, demanding that they stick to the £20 per week wage I had been promised. Unfortunately, my refusal meant that I had to carry on packing cardigans and jumpers a while longer!

I then applied for a job with the British Motor Corporation (BMC). A fellow Prague player, a cockney called John Bond, already worked there. I was successful in being offered a post and started in April 1964. I worked there for the rest of the time I was in Australia. I didn't particularly like it, but it got me that £20 per week. The role was in supply and production control, working in the office of the Sheet Metal and Body Division (SMBD), where they made the Mini. I had to make sure that there was a constant supply line of parts needed to build the cars, otherwise I got my backside kicked. That did happen at times, not through any fault of mine, but because suppliers were failing to meet their schedule.

Each year, the SMBD played a very competitive rugby league game against another department called CKD, which was where the cars were finished. In 1965, the organiser for my department came into the office, asking some members of staff if they wanted to play in the game. When he was about to leave, I said, "You haven't asked me if I want to play."

He replied, "You soccer players are too soft to play rugby league."

This was the *Sheilas, Wogs and Poofters* attitude in action. The rugby match was due to be played on the Saturday, and although Prague had an important game on the Sunday, my response to the organiser was, "Pick me, and I'll play." He put my name down on his list and passed it on to the captain of the team, who did then pick me. I explained to the captain of the SMBD team that I couldn't be expected to tackle the big guys, but not to worry about me for the rest of the game. At the one training session I attended, he gave me a coaching lesson on how I might tackle if I had to.

On the day of the game, the captain decided that I would play outside-centre. There were two wingers and two centres in the team – the outside-centre was the one who played on the left-hand side. It was a tight game, and I was not too involved in it until early in the second half, when I received the ball behind the posts in my "in goal area". I ran the full length of the pitch – 105 metres! The opposition couldn't catch me – I was just too quick for them. I ran past them, through them, round them, over the top of them, and touched down for the try between the posts at the other end of the pitch! It was extraordinary. I scored another try later in the game at the same end, which helped us to win the game 12–9. I was the toast of the SMBD, as far as rugby league was concerned! I didn't claim to be as good as Reg Gasnier (who played centre for St George Dragons, and by reputation is probably Australia's greatest ever centre), but then again, my rugby league record is played one, won one, scored two tries! I'm very proud to have stood up for myself and my fellow soccer players.

I was fine for the Prague match the next day. I hadn't been tackled playing rugby, and I think I only tackled one person. Even that was jumping on a guy when someone else had already brought him down!

While I was working at BMC, Lesley was found secretarial work in a car sales showroom, which she enjoyed. The showroom was in the Kings Cross suburb of Sydney, which at that time was also the red-light district of the city!

At Prague, I had the same schedule as I'd had with Wigan: I worked full-time Monday to Friday, then had football training on Tuesday and Thursday evenings and a match on Saturday or Sunday. Prague was more or less the top team in Australia when I got there, but they were on the wane slightly. As I mentioned earlier, in 1959, the club were banned for signing players from Austria and Hungary who were still in contract with other clubs. That ban was lifted in 1964, and after that, they got some good players. In fact, I was very surprised by the quality of the players. There were over 20 different nationalities playing in Australia then, and that also really surprised me. I wasn't used to that, of course, as in the UK, the players were all from England, Ireland, Scotland or Wales. Over in Australia, as well as players from the UK, they had some from Austria, Yugoslavia, Spain, Argentina, Brazil, Holland, Belgium, China, Germany, Hungary, Czechoslovakia, Italy, Greece, Poland, Uruguay, Malta, Egypt, South Africa, and of course Australia. The skill of the Argentinians and Europeans was fantastic, and certainly much better than us "poms". Nobby Badaracco and Luis Gauto taught me how to nutmeg people, which means putting the ball between someone's legs when they try to challenge you and running past them. Back then, that was unheard of in English football. What the English players were good at was tackling people, being hard and whacking the ball up front! We had a will to chase the ball that the Europeans didn't. The English style was "wham, bam, kick and slam". Compared to other English players, I was quite skilful in controlling and passing the ball, but learning from the foreign players during my time in Australia was a really important part of my footballing education.

I mentioned Yugoslavia as one of the nationalities playing in Australia at the time. I quickly learnt that the Croats and the Serbs were very different people, and they didn't love each other, to say the least. In fact, not long after we arrived, there was an instance of letter-bombing in the street next to where we lived in Marrickville. I'm not sure whether the victim was Serb or Croat, but I do know that a man's hand was blown off. When the police went to investigate, they were told by the victim and his friends, "Don't worry about it, we'll deal with it." As a result of this, a team called Croatia were made to change their name to Metropolitan Adriatic. The name was only changed for a year and was done to take the situation away from the news headlines.

A player called Brian Green had come over to Australia from the UK around the same time as me, but he only stayed for a couple of months. We knew him as "Greeny"; he was a big centre-forward but couldn't get into the team. One night at training, we were lying on the pitch doing some sit-ups and we could see the planes flying overhead, coming into land at the nearby Sydney International Airport. Brian said, "I'm going to be on one of them next week." I asked what he meant, and he told me he was going home. "But you've got a three-year contract to fulfil," I reminded him.

"I'm going home," he insisted. I'll tell them my dad's died."

A week later, I went to training and asked where Greeny was. "He had to go home," they told me. "His dad's died."

Bizarrely, that turned out to be the truth! His dad had actually died that week. The next time I saw him, I said, "I bet your dad didn't realise that you'd put his name down as payment for you leaving Australia."

When I started my training with Prague, they had just won the Ampol Cup, a pre-season cup sponsored by the Ampol petrol company. However, I soon realised that my own personal prospects were not necessarily as rosy as the club had first implied. They already had the best left-winger in Australia, the Argentinian player called Luis Gauto that I mentioned before, and I would be competing with him and other skilful players for a place in the team. The first league game of the season, which took place a couple of weeks after I arrived, was against a team called Budapest St George. Fortunately for me, Luis Gauto had been injured in a pre-season friendly, and I played in the game. A *Daily Mirror* newspaper report after the match said:

Prague Stem Spirited Finish

Prague soccer team yesterday beat Budapest St George 4–3, after Budapest staged a fighting finish to score two goals in the last five minutes at the Sydney Athletic Field. Brian Tristram scored two goals and was always in position. Prague's new outside left, Geoff Sleight, gave a good first match display, and was unlucky not to score when one of his shots rebounded off the goalpost and hit the other post.

That was a good start. I see my first season with Prague, which was a relatively successful one, as the beginning of my reinvention. However, my season was cut short by three

63

games when I had an altercation with the Prague captain. His name was Les Scheinflug, and one day in training, I kicked him. I was in a bad mood that day, and I must admit that the kick was deliberate, but I disguised it in the form of a tackle. This very strong-willed German turned and said to me, "You kick me again, I vill kill you (*sic*)".

Without being xenophobic, this was happening less than 20 years since the end of the Second World War, and the English and the Germans didn't get on. Although I suppose, at the time, I assumed that having a bossy and aggressive reaction to one simple kick was just what Germans were like. I had no reason to think anything different. I now know that's not true, and in fact, Les became a good friend of mine! However, back when I was 20 and he said he would kill me, I behaved exactly as the 20-year-old Geoff Sleight would. I decided to test his promise, so as soon as he got the ball again, I kicked him! As he went for me, I swiped him one in the face. Before Les could get to me, the lads all jumped on him. While they were pulling him away, I made it 2–0 by punching him again.

When the Australian soccer season finished in October, I knew that I wasn't going to resume training until the pre-season Ampol Cup the following February. What was I going to do in the meantime? Well, I still weighed 11 stone at the time, so I decided to go on a diet. From the diet of steak, chips, cheese and beer which had caused me to put weight on, I switched to having a tin of baked beans and some stewed steak every night for dinner. Through that summer, I got my weight back down to 10 stone, and that meant when I went back to pre-season training, I could "catch pigeons" again.

My speed was back. Now, my reinvention really was under way.

We started the Ampol Cup the following year. In the quarter-final, we beat Hakoah; in the semi-final, we beat Apia; then in the final, we were due to play Yugal. We went for a pre-match meal at a really posh place called Dunbar House up near Bondi. Prague was a very sociable club and would hold two or three dinner dances at Dunbar House every year for the players – it was really nice. During the meal, one of the directors was sent over to my table to tell me that I wasn't playing in the final. The coach, Stefan Cambal, was a Czechoslovakian who had played for his country in the World Cup of 1938. Unfortunately, he couldn't really speak English, so he'd sent a director to tell me the news. In sheer annoyance, I stood up and tipped the table over!

The team won the final 6–2 without me. Did that justify the coach's decision? I suppose the answer has to be yes. However, I was never dropped again throughout the rest of my time in Australia. The coach thought that I was a very good player, and, as he learnt to speak a bit of English, he thanked me personally on a number of occasions.

International Games

In May 1965, after the season finished in England, Chelsea then came on tour to Australia. The tendency wasn't to play clubs on these types of tours, but to play representative teams from each state, such as New South Wales or Victoria. Regardless, a match was scheduled between the Australian national team and Chelsea in Melbourne. Out of the blue, I got a letter saying that I had been added to the national squad, with a ticket to fly down to Melbourne! It was a total shock to me. I didn't play – there were no substitutes – but I went down to watch the game as part of the squad.

I returned to Prague, and then played in a game against the German team VFB Stuttgart. That was memorable because Tommy Docherty, the Chelsea manager, played for Prague as a guest. The *Green Football Paper* reported on the match as follows:

VFB Stuttgart & Prague Put On A Fine Show

The 6,000 spectators who braved last Tuesday night's bitter cold will remember the Prague vs VFB Stuttgart match as one of the best international fixtures ever played in Sydney. The exhilarating match was more exciting and produced far better soccer than any of the matches of Chelsea's current tour. Stuttgart beat Prague 3–1, but at no stage was the Sydney team ever outclassed. Actually, Prague had as much of the ball as

66

the Germans, and their display did not pale in comparison with their skilful opponents. Prague lifted their game, as they always do on big occasions, playing their best football this year. VFB Stuttgart thrilled the crowd with their fast, direct methods. They impressed fans as the hardest shooting overseas team seen in Sydney, and were always dangerous when attacking. Their first two goals were magnificent, but the third one, three minutes before full-time, was the result of a scramble and could easily have been avoided by Prague's defence. For Prague, none played better than young stopper Zeman, left-winger Geoff Sleight, who scored a superb goal which lifted Prague's hopes, and full-back Freddy Falzon. Tommy Docherty, the Chelsea coach who filled a guest spot, inspired the Prague defence and is "still a great player at 36 years of age," said the VFB Stuttgart coach after the match.

What the article doesn't say is that it was Tommy Docherty who gave away the third goal! My goal was a good one. Until I read that report again recently, I didn't remember just how good a match it was.

After that, I played in other representative games, including one for New South Wales against an Israeli team called Hapoel. In August 1965, the Soccer Federation of Australia (SFA) decided to enter the World Cup, having been banned for the previous five years, as I've mentioned before. The draw was made for the group stage, and South Korea and North Korea were drawn in the same group. South Korea refused to play North Korea and withdrew. South Africa were also named in the group, but they had been banned from taking part because of Apartheid. That just left North Korea and Australia to fight it out.

The first match against North Korea was due to be played in Cambodia in November 1965. As the conditions there would be hot and humid, it was decided to take the squad to Cairns in northern Queensland for a month in order to acclimatise. In my opinion, our Yugoslavian coach Tiko Jelisavčić made a mistake in taking 21 of us, because only 20 players could go to the World Cup. I was certainly worried about becoming that 21st player who didn't get to go, and everyone else must have been thinking the same thing.

In order to play for Australia, we had to be Australian citizens. Of the 21 in the squad, 12 of us were British, but if you were a pom, you could apply for citizenship after 12 months of residency in the country. If you were a European, Greek or Italian, for example, you had to have three or five years of residency in order to gain citizenship. A fellow Brit in the squad had only been in Australia for eight months, so he became the one who couldn't go to Cambodia. If the rest of us had known things were going to work out that way, we would have enjoyed the month-long training camp in Cairns a lot more! At the time, I thought it was a poor way to have managed the preparation, and I still think so now.

During our preparation in Cairns, it also became clear that not all of the players in the squad were fit enough. We were all part-time professionals, whereas it later came to our attention that our upcoming opponents, North Korea, had played 35 international games in the previous three years. Their players were also all in the North Korean army and had spent the last two years in Russia. Some of our players trained harder than others, but our actual training programme was not structured to achieve any standard of fitness that would be comparable to today's standards. We did some running for fitness, but apart from that, it was very poor or virtually non-existent. There was also no organisation on set plays, such as corners and free kicks, for or against. In fact, there was not even an acknowledgement of the need for set plays to be practised. There was no consideration given to technique or the shape of the team; the players involved simply brought their own technique and skills if they had them. Most importantly of all, there was little camaraderie, togetherness or team spirit. There were cliques within the group, including a split between "probables" and "possibles", and players who came from the same club side tended to stick together.

We all know more about preparation nowadays than we did

then, but it's important to recognise that without these first efforts at training camps and acclimatisation (however successful or otherwise), subsequent developments would not have followed.

When we got to Cambodia, our training sessions during the week before the first match consisted of full-scale practice games. The teams were made up of the 11 "probables" against the 9 "possibles", plus the coach and a local Cambodian player. The North Koreans, who had trained on the same pitch as us earlier in the day, stayed behind to watch us play these games. I know it sounds crazy, but that's what happened! Dave Todd and I, a fellow Brit who is still a good friend of mine, must have taken the opportunity to show something good in those games, because when the team was announced for the first game, we were both included. Despite the shortcomings of our preparations, we still felt that we had done enough and would beat North Korea.

The first game was played in Phnom Penh on 21st November 1965. History shows that North Korea won the game 6–1, which was a good hiding for us. There are contributory factors (which should probably not be recorded in writing at this stage), but I know that any attempt to make the result look better just looks like an excuse.

On the coach going back to the hotel, the atmosphere was similar to that of a morgue. In an effort to make things feel

70

better, I said that things could have been worse; that if we hadn't scored, we would have lost 0–6. I also had a 1–6 scoreline in the sweep! My bet had actually been on a 6–1 win for us, but the others had felt that was such an outrageous suggestion that they had let me have it on both teams. I won the sweep – every cloud has a silver lining! Understandably, the SFA President Jim Bayutti, who was on the coach with us, was less than pleased and made some comment to that effect. My intention was just to cheer everybody up, but I now realise that wasn't my job.

However, that first loss didn't mean it was all over. The matches were not played on an aggregate score principle, but instead on points: two points for a win, one point for a draw and nothing if you lost. Due to the points-based system, goal difference didn't count; if Australia won the second game, even just 1–0, we would be level and go to a third match play-off.

Between the first and second matches, I openly said that I felt 1–3 would have been a fairer result. Some of the lads felt that if we scored first in the second match, we would beat North Korea, but I disagreed. The second game took place on 24th November. In the end, we did score the first goal in the second match, but then went on to lose 1–3. I'm still of the opinion that this scoreline is a fairer representation of the difference in quality between the two teams. Whatever way you look at it, they were better than we were.

Following the second game against North Korea, having been eliminated from the World Cup, a game was arranged for us against Cambodia. All members of the squad played at least one half of the match. I thought it was a friendly, but it was actually registered with FIFA as an official international match, which finished as a 0–0 draw.

We then played a number of further games in the Far East, improving considerably in each. Initially, we travelled to Hong Kong, where we were beaten 0–1. In the second game in Hong Kong, we beat a Swedish club 3–2. We then played against Taiwan. As their biggest rivals, Hong Kong, had beaten us, Chinese gamblers staked a lot of money on Taiwan also beating us. However, we won the match (I don't recall the score), and that led to serious riots outside the ground after the final whistle. We were all in the dressing room, and there were dustbins being thrown through the windows and riot police everywhere.

The following day, we flew to Ipoh to play two games against the Malaysian national team. We won the games 1–0 and 3–0. Having not played in Hong Kong or Ipoh, I spoke privately to Tiko and asked him why I wasn't being selected. He said that he had been instructed not to play me again, but that he would make it up to me in the future. Obviously, I was not happy, especially being such a long way from home and not

72

being able to do anything about it. I suspected the problem was to do with Jim Bayutti, the president.

In the *Green Football Paper,* the journalist Lou Gautier, who was on the tour with us, reported that, "Geoff Sleight became the forgotten man on the tour, having been the best winger on view in the build-up to the first game." I have a copy of that article in my scrapbook and asked Lou about it some years later, but he wouldn't comment any further.

We returned to Australia at the beginning of December, and pre-season began again in February 1966. After playing in the Ampol Cup and being named in the *Green Football Paper*'s "Team of the Tournament", I started the season on fire. We beat Hakoah, the team Tiko Jelisavčić coached, 3–1 at Wentworth Park in the first game.

In June 1966, Tiko had to pick a team for the New South Wales game against the Italian team AS Roma, who were on tour in Australia at the time. Tiko picked six Apia players, four Hakoah players, and Geoff Sleight from Prague! That was Tiko making it up to me, as he had promised back in Malaysia. I really respected him for keeping his word. The president of New South Wales was John Thomson, not Jim Bayutti, and so Tiko was free to select me. Unfortunately, Roma won the game 2–1. The report of the game in the *Green Football Paper* said:

> Danny Walsh found the "flying" Sleight with a perfect long pass. The winger dribbled past two defenders and

crossed the ball for Campana to equalise. Geoff Sleight was the only New South Wales forward to trouble the AS Roma defence.

AS Roma played Australia the following week. Jim Bayutti was still the president, with Frank Parsons having replaced Tiko as the coach. Once again, Bayutti prevented the coach from selecting me for the team. Bruce Morrow from Newcastle played wide on the right in a 1–1 draw. You can draw your own conclusions, but I'm not going to criticise Parsons or Morrow, as I didn't know them.

Now, many years later and with the benefit of hindsight, I can say that I would still do it all again, just to be a member of Australia's first World Cup team. History can't be changed, and if, God willing, Australia do win the World Cup in future, I will still be proud to have been there at the beginning. Nobody, not even Jim Bayutti, can change that! I can laugh and talk about the experience now.

"Socceroo" is the term, imaginatively coined by a *Daily Mirror* journalist, to describe members of the Australian national team, based on the fact they play soccer and the country has kangaroos! I'm proud to have been a Socceroo.

Not many of the other squad members from that first World Cup game will remember the details of my subsequent deselection, but I do because it happened to me. I didn't think I would mention this story again, because neither Tiko nor Jim

Bayutti are still alive. I was hesitant about telling the story here, because I didn't want to comment on people who weren't in a position to give their side of things. However, a very dear friend of mine, Melanie, who is a barrister, has advised me that you cannot defame the dead, so that's why it's here!

My three contracted seasons in Australia were all a massive learning curve. I never telephoned home from Australia in the whole time I was there, as it would have cost £1 per minute. Instead, I used to send an airmail letter to my mother every week and would look forward to her reply. The world was very different back then – communication was much more difficult. I couldn't even watch England win the 1966 World Cup Final, as there were no satellites in the sky to enable television to be broadcast around the world. I listened to the game on the radio in the middle of the night!

For a long time, I didn't enjoy being in Australia. I was a long way from home and was looking forward to getting back to the UK. I was missing my mates – although, as I later found out, they weren't missing me as much, because of course they were all still together. In fact, I wanted to come home so much that I drew a little chart of how many days it was before my contract was up. When I drew the chart, it was 981 days away, and each day, I scribbled off a square. Fortunately, as we stayed there longer, I did get used to it, and by the time we left, I liked it a lot more than I had when I first arrived.

However, I still didn't ever consider renewing my contract. All the way through, Lesley and I planned to come back to the UK. That was slightly unusual, though, because lots of people stayed. People often anglicised their names, like one of the club's owners, George Verner, who anglicised his name to Warner, and his descendants were born Australians. For the vast majority of people who migrated to Australia, that was how it went – that's how Australia grew and developed. Many people moved there for a minimum of two years but didn't ever go back and went on to have children there. When I first arrived, I think there was something like 3 million people in Sydney and 2 million people in Melbourne. Now there's over 5 million people in each of those cities, and over 25 million in Australia as a whole.

At that point, I never had any intention of becoming an Aussie and living there permanently. Our lives in Australia were always run on the knowledge that we were going home after three seasons. Of course, I subsequently *did* become an Aussie, but that was for a different reason.

By the end of the 1966 season, Prague had lost most of their best players. We had a poor finish to the season and lost our last five games, although I was named in the "Team of the Season" by the *Green Football Paper*, and still have a copy as evidence. My three contracted seasons were up, and it was time to think about what I was going to do in the future.

We sailed home on the *Oriana*, departing on 26th September and landing back in England on 21st October 1966. Unfortunately, when I got back up north and met up with my friends, the ones I had been missing and trying to keep in touch with via airmail letters, I found that we had little to talk about. They had grown up over the three years I'd been away, as I had, and while they might be interested in hearing about Australia for a couple of minutes, they weren't interested in listening to me talk about it all the time. I think they had been pleased for me when I became a professional footballer, and when I moved first to Bolton and then to Australia, but in my time away, I had dropped out of the group. When they were still meeting up for a few pints or going away to Blackpool for a few days, I doubt that they were saying, "I wonder what Geoff's up to in Sydney?" I had been thinking about them every day, but my experience when I got back told me that they hadn't been thinking about me too much, although Graham Kyte had written to me on a few occasions.

One of the good things about the money we had earnt in Australia was that not only had I been able to pay the £400 cost of us both getting home, but I was also able to put down a £1,050 deposit on a three-bedroom detached house that cost £2,650. It doesn't sound like much money now, but my contemporaries were having to borrow money from their parents to be able to get a £200 deposit together. All through our time in Australia, every time I got that win bonus, we were saving and saving. Interestingly, when I went to borrow the outstanding £1,600 to buy the house, I was offered a choice of taking a fixed interest rate of 6.5% or having a variable rate. Not knowing much about it, I said that I would accept the fixed rate. Shortly after I made that decision in 1967, inflation rocketed – by 1982, the interest rate was 14.4%. Lesley still lives in that house in Royston, and it's now worth about £230,000. I just got lucky by accidentally making the right call to take the fixed rate, but I'm pleased to say that it's all part of my sons' inheritance.

Figure 14 Flat 9, 340 Marrickville Road, Marrickville, Sydney. Home in Sydney 1964-1966.

Figure 15 Australian World Cup squad in Cairns for acclimatisation, October 1965. I am in the front row, far left.

Figure 16 Leaving for Cambodia to play North Korea, Kingsford Smith Airport, Sydney, November 1965.

Figure 17 Australian World Cup squad leaving for Cambodia to play against North Korea in World Cup Qualifier, November 1965.

Figure 18 Leaving Sydney in 1965 to play against North Korea in Cambodia.

Figure 19 Sydney FC Prague, 30th January 1966. i am in the front row, far right.

Figure 20 In action in Australia with Archie Blue, Prague versus Apia, 1966.

Figure 21 New South Wales versus AS Roma, June 1966. I am in the front row, far left.

CHAPTER FIVE

A Second Reinvention

I had reinvented myself as a footballer by going to Australia and losing the excess weight I had been carrying. I was now back to where I'd started before I signed for Bolton: I didn't have a job and I didn't have a football club. At the age of 23, it was time for another reinvention!

I had met some friends in Australia who lived in Bristol. After a week at home, I got myself a month-long trial at Bristol Rovers. Their manager, Bert Tann, was a real gentleman. After a fortnight he was rubbing his hands, happy at the left-winger he had found. The second fortnight, unfortunately, didn't work out quite so well. Mr Tann called me in and said that although I was as good as his existing left-winger, he needed me to be a lot better than him if I was to be offered a contract. Perhaps I hadn't shown my full potential because I'd just come off three weeks on a boat, doing no training. Nowadays when I go on a cruise, I'm in the gym every day!

I still thought I could find myself an opportunity in Bristol, so I got a temporary job nearby at the British Aircraft Corporation (BAC). During my five weeks there, the company were building the Concorde, a very prestigious supersonic passenger jet. I had a small role in ordering supplies and ensuring they were delivered on time. I used to come out of the office and watch as the plane was being built, bit by bit. Funnily enough nowadays, when I go on holiday to Barbados, there is a decommissioned Concorde at the international airport there.

After that, I came back up to Yorkshire and got a job in the education department of the West Riding County Council, as a clerical officer. I was back at the bottom of the pile, and I wasn't happy to be there. My contemporaries in age were five years ahead of me in work experience and climbing up the pay scale.

I decided to enrol at Wakefield Technical and Art College on a four-year course. If I passed each year, I would earn a Diploma in Municipal Administration (DMA). The course encompassed local government, central government and the associated services. I continued to work full-time in the education department, but went to college on day release, plus two evenings a week. I can talk about it now and enjoy talking about it, but I didn't enjoy it at the time. It was such hard work; it was right on the margins of my ability.

That decision was motivated by two factors. Firstly, to pass the people in front of me. Secondly, Lesley was pregnant, so I was now the only earner in the household. On £14 per week, with a baby on the way and my wife not working, I was a long way behind what I had been earning years before, when I first went to Bolton.

I passed the first year and was then given two increments,

which helped. The second year was called the intermediate stage and it was a qualification itself, the Intermediate DMA. When I passed that, it gave me a minimum salary of £860 per year. I was progressing.

The next two years, final part one and final part two, were really hard. The course reduced from six subjects down to three subjects. The first year had been equivalent to O Level, and the second year was more like A Level. By the final year, it was approaching degree level. A lot of the students dropped out along the way, but there were around 12 of us who formed a strong, competitive group. I'm competitive in everything I do, so that helped me. We would hand in a piece of work and it would then be strictly marked by the college staff. Whoever scored bottom in that particular essay would be slaughtered by the others. We really tormented them by constantly reminding them how bad they were. That provided motivation for all of us to make sure that we weren't the one who finished bottom in the next assignment. It raised the standards overall, and we all ended up with a Diploma in Municipal Administration.

When I had completed the course, I could go on further and continue studying. I replied in my own Yorkshire language that I wouldn't be: "Thanks, but no thanks!" By the time I had completed the fourth year, I was guaranteed an annual salary of £1,200, which was a big jump up from where I had started.

Very fortunately for me, in 1974 there was an overhaul of the local government system. It's the biggest change there has ever been in local government – the changes did away with some regions entirely. The West Riding of Yorkshire didn't exist anymore and was instead split up into several different authorities. I was on £2,100 by then, and during the reorganisation, I got a new job at Barnsley on £2,850.

Non-League Football

While all this was happening, I was also playing non-league football and getting a bit of extra income there too. Paul, my first son, had been born on 22nd March 1968. I didn't play football at all that season. A lot of that was caused by the outbreak of foot and mouth disease among livestock, which caused matches to be cancelled. With a family to support, I realised that I had to supplement my income further, so I worked in Windsor's bookmakers on Saturdays during this time. After my spell at Bristol Rovers, I had a similar short stint at Barnsley. It was the same situation of having to be a better player than the guys they already had. However, even before the trial had finished, I told the manager to forget about offering me a full-time contract. My plan was to go part-time and play non-league football while working, as I had done with Wigan before I left for Australia.

The nearest non-league club that paid any amount of money

was Stalybridge Celtic. However, it was very little money and it wasn't very near either — it was a 35-mile drive across the Pennines. The manager there was Colin Whitaker, a former professional footballer with Queens Park Rangers, Sheffield Wednesday, Shrewsbury Town, Bradford Park Avenue, Oldham and Rochdale. I wrote to Colin, and two days later, I hadn't heard back from him. So, I got in the car and drove over to Stalybridge football ground. It was a Tuesday, and I knew that they trained on Tuesdays and Thursdays. I asked if the manager was in and was told that he was out on the pitch. I walked down the tunnel, out onto the pitch, and into the middle of the training session. I said, "Are you Colin Whitaker? I'm Geoff Sleight. I wrote to you and asked you for a trial, but you haven't replied."

I didn't realise at the time, but as well as being the Stalybridge manager, Colin co-owned a sports shop called Whitaker and Green. The Green in the partnership was Brian Green, the "Greeny" I had played football with briefly at Sydney FC Prague! When I found that out, I realised that Colin would check what Brian had to say about me before getting back to me. Brian must have assured Colin that I could play, because after a couple of training sessions, he signed me for Stalybridge Celtic.

I commuted 35 miles each way on Tuesday and Thursday nights, and travelled to wherever we were playing on the

Saturday. I was paid £7 per week, plus expenses. In my first two years there, we finished fifth and then third in the Cheshire League, which was much higher than the club had ever previously finished. Also, in my second year there, we won the Manchester Intermediate Cup.

Colin Whitaker was then offered a job at Altrincham, which was a step up, and he asked me to go with him. However, this caused some trouble. The club found out that Colin had tapped me up (approached me with the offer), and as a direct result, they refused to release Colin from his contract. It ended up in court.

Colin asked me if I would support him in court, and I said I would. On the day itself, I stood in the dock and faced a barrister who said, "You play for Stalybridge. You were approached by the manager to go to Altrincham. You said you would go."

I just looked at him.

The barrister said, "Well?"

I replied, "Well what?"

"Well, is that true?"

"Oh, I thought you were telling me, not asking me!"

I don't know how I got away with that! The judge pulled it all to a conclusion and said that he wasn't willing to have another day of arguing in court – both parties had to go out and reach a conclusion between themselves. In the end, Stalybridge agreed to let Colin go, but wouldn't release me. Altrincham withdrew their offer to Colin, but Buxton then offered him a job instead. There was a quote from a reporter called Terry Gorry in the *Manchester Evening News* which said:

Geoff Sleight said, "I played for the manager. I did not play for the club."

I had said that to the reporter. It probably didn't please the board of directors much to hear it, but it was true. I played for Colin, and I didn't want to stay at Stalybridge if he wasn't there. The club got a new manager in called Dick Walker. He was a decent guy, but he wasn't from a professional football level. Nevertheless, I stayed for one more season at Stalybridge and my wages were increased to £10 per week because I stayed. We finished sixth in the league that season, with Buxton finishing eighth. George Smith, who was the Stalybridge goalkeeper, then became manager of the club when Dick Walker was released. I told George that I wanted to go to Buxton and asked if he would release me from my contract. He agreed, saying that he didn't want to keep anybody at the club who didn't want to play for him.

Once I was released from Stalybridge, I signed for Buxton. When I got there, I asked Colin if he was going to give me a pay rise for making the move. He wouldn't, and I stayed on the same £10 per week! Plus, my trips to Buxton were 45 miles each way, so even further than I'd been travelling for Stalybridge.

In my first season for Buxton, 1971/72, we made it to the final of the Derbyshire Senior Cup. It was heading towards the end of the season and we knew we weren't going to win the Cheshire League, but we still had two league games left to play. Colin got all the players together and said, "We've had a decent season, but you're playing for your places in the cup final now."

"Just a minute," I replied, "I've played 50-odd games this season and I've played well, but you're saying that if I have a couple of not-so-good games now, then I'm not getting to play in the final?"

"That's right." Colin said.

Some of the lads weren't pleased at this, but I went mad. After the way I'd played all season, I felt that it would be unfair if I was dropped for the final, regardless of how the next two games went. We played the last two league games, finished fourth in the table overall, and I was picked for the final, but I still wasn't happy.

The final was over two legs, with the winner decided on aggregate score. We were playing Matlock and the first leg was at Buxton's home ground. We ran them ragged through sheer annoyance and won 4–0. As I walked back into the dressing room and threw my boots into the corner, I asked

90

Colin, "Are you satisfied now?"

"No," he said. "We've a second leg still to play."

The following week, we had a lovely April evening to go to Matlock for the second leg. At half time, the score was 2–0 to Matlock. We were given a bit of a talking to by Colin during the break. Five minutes into the second half, Buxton won a penalty. I took the ball and put it on the spot. I must have taken at least a 12-yard run-up, and then smacked the ball inside the left-hand post. That did it – the result was settled, and we won 5–2 on aggregate.

The first thing I said to Colin when I got back to the dressing room after the final whistle was, "Are you satisfied *now*?"

Colin replied, "Yeah, it was a great penalty you took."

"It wasn't a problem for me," I said. "I imagined your head was just inside the post, and as far as I'm concerned, I hit you right in the face with the ball."

Despite this, Colin and I got on well. The other players used to call me "midge" because I was small. I knew that the great goal scorer Malcolm Macdonald was nicknamed "Super Mac", so I decided to call myself "Super Midge"! Terry Gorry had an article in the *Manchester Evening News* around this time that read:

> Buxton boss Colin Whitaker found himself with a minor
> domestic problem when he "signed on" a cat to take on a

team of mice that had invaded his home. His three boys wondered what the new striker (the cat) should be named, but when the new boy arrived and turned out to be the smallest in its squad (the smallest kitten in the litter), the problem was solved. He was promptly named Super Midge, *after the nickname of the smallest player in the Buxton squad, 5ft 4in left-half Geoff Sleight. Sleight said modestly, "That means it should be fast enough to catch the mice!"*

I started the next season, 1972/73, still doing the same travelling back and forth to Buxton. Luckily, I had company, because I used to give a lift to a teammate called Mick Pamment, who I would pick up near Holmfirth. We had a good team with a couple of new players and won the Cheshire League comfortably with a few games to go. However, after winning the league, we then lost three finals. Since then, I've always said that if we hadn't won the league so early, we would have won those three finals as well. We probably relaxed too soon, having achieved the main target. On paper, it still looks good to have reached three finals and won the league, but it was disappointing to experience. We also got to the last eight of the FA Challenge Trophy, which was a new national non-league competition. We thought we had a chance of winning it, or at least playing in the final at Wembley, but it wasn't to be. Stafford Rangers were very good at that time, and they won it instead.

Due to winning the Cheshire League, at the start of the 1973/74 season, we had gained promotion to the Northern Premier League, which was a comparatively new tier that had started in 1969. This was now the top non-league division in the country – we were in it with the so-called "big boys". We did OK and held a position about halfway up the table. We weren't going to win it, but we weren't going to be relegated either.

One snowy Tuesday evening in February, I headed over to training in Buxton. Going over the Pennines in the snow is not a great idea, but I made it. When I got there, however, we found the pitch was unplayable. Colin Whitaker told us to go for a run instead. We ran off down the hill in the dark, up through town for a couple of miles, and then headed back. There were around five players in the team who came from nearby Sheffield, and they had formed a bit of a clique. On the way back from the run, I saw a couple of them standing at the bottom of the hill near the ground, having a fag. They hadn't gone on the run at all! I thought, *I'm not having this*. I went in to see Colin and although I didn't mention any names, I told him that he'd better sort it out. "I'm not driving over here in the snow to go running in the dark, while they stand about smoking," I told him. "If you haven't sorted it out by Thursday, I'm not coming to training, and if it isn't sorted by Saturday,

I'm not playing then, either."

I was true to my word – I refused to play until the issue was resolved and I was suspended without pay as a result, at first for two weeks. Terry Gorry, the journalist, used to call me up quite regularly, and the next time I spoke to him, I told him what was going on. On 2nd March, he ran an article in the *Manchester Evening News* under the headline: "50p petrol starts walk-out protest." He chose to present the story as a protest about how much it was costing me to travel over there. In part it was, but I only objected to spending that time and money travelling when others were getting away with not training at all.

I kept refusing to play, and Buxton kept suspending me for a further two weeks each time, until the end of the season. Colin said that if I didn't back down, then he wouldn't release me at the end of the season, meaning that I couldn't go and play for any other club either. I told him, "In that case, I'll retire." On principle, I wasn't going to give in because I knew I was in the right. Perhaps Colin thought that taking action against five players would weaken the team too much, but whatever the reason, he refused to act against them and we had a major fall-out. I didn't play for Buxton again.

At the end of the season, Buxton relented and did release me from my contract. It was now April, and I hadn't played since February. Then, a manager called Bob Murphy from Mossley rang me and asked to come and see me because he was interested in signing me. I didn't know Bob at all, since he'd come out of the local leagues as a manager rather than being an ex-player. He came to my house and we had a chat. I found him to be a very straight, honest guy and we got on well. He said that he wanted to sign me and that he would pay me £20 per week, which was more than I'd been on at Buxton. I told Bob that I wasn't fit and would need to train hard pre-season to be ready, but I was willing to do that. I also reminded him that I had been released by Buxton and was therefore a free agent, so if I found out he had paid Buxton any money for me, I wouldn't play for him. He replied, "You'll find out, Geoff, that I say what I mean, and mean what I say."

Bob was brilliant – he trained us hard, but he was very good at his job. Mossley also played in the Northern Premier League, and in October, we had to play Buxton at our home ground. It was a Wednesday night game, and they beat us 2–3. I went into the bar after the match to have a drink before heading home. When I walked in, I was careful to ignore Colin Whitaker, who I could see was sitting nearby. As I passed his chair, I heard his voice say, "Ask Sleighty if he wants a drink."

I shouted out, "Tell him Sleighty doesn't want a drink!" and I went to buy myself a drink.

The following week, we had to play Buxton again, this time at their home ground. We beat them 1–0. I walked into their bar after the game and called out, "Ask Whit if he wants a drink!"

He replied, "Yeah, I'll have a pint of bitter." That was Colin all over, and that was the end to all the tension between us. We made up.

As he got older, Colin Whitaker sadly developed dementia. He passed away in May 2015 and his wife, Sue, asked me to speak at his funeral. At first, I wasn't sure if I could, but I agreed. This is the eulogy I delivered to the packed church:

> This is the biggest crowd that I've played in front of for many years. A testimony to the love and respect that we all had for our friend, Colin Whitaker. I could talk all afternoon telling you stories about Whit, and I'd be happy to do just that. However, after a lot of consideration and soul-searching, I realise that it is impossible to do him justice in the limited time available. So, I would just like to read to you a very condensed insight into a pal that I first met 47 years ago.
>
> *Although Whit lived most of his life in Lancashire, you will know that he actually hailed from Pudsey near Leeds, which means that he was made up of 100% Yorkshire DNA, which in turn means that he had an innate inability to understand the concept of finishing second in anything that he did. In other words, he was not the best of losers. Being a fellow Yorkshireman, I understand perfectly how he felt, and if that is considered by anyone to be a flaw in*

his character, then all I can say is that none of us are perfect anyway. Even Jesus is reported to have lost his temper with the moneylenders in the temple!

As far as I'm concerned, Whit was a winner in every aspect of his life. In his role as a father and family man, in his role as a businessman, and in his role as a sportsman. He was a generous man, and he had a wicked sense of humour, but it would also be remiss of me if I didn't say that he could be as grumpy as hell at the prospect of getting a silver medal, whether it be in football, squash, golf or even in an argument. If any of you can recall him giving you a let at squash, or a putt at golf, you ought to come up here in the pulpit and tell us all about it. He really did think that being second was the first of the losers. He was a winner.

Sadly, Whit has been taken from us. In football parlance, he has played and lost his last game. But he didn't go down without a fight, because he had Sue in his corner to nurse him and care for him through his darkest days during the past three or four years. In reality, he was like a big brother to me, and my life has been enriched by having Colin Whitaker as a friend. On behalf of everybody here today, goodbye Whit, rest in peace and God bless you.

I didn't quite make it to the end of the last sentence because

I had a tear in my eye. We all went to the wake at the golf club later, and these two women came up to me and said, "That was lovely, what you said about Colin. When we saw that tear run down your face, we all started crying!" Whit was 11 years older than me, so was 82 when he died. Our similar characters – never being willing to give in – is probably what he liked about me.

Figure 22 Stalybridge Celtic, 1968/69 winners of the Manchester Intermediate Cup, I am in the front row, third from the right.

Figure 23 Stalybridge Celtic. I am in the front row, third from the right.

Figure 24 My older son Paul, mascot at Stalybridge Celtic, 1970/71.

Figure 25 Buxton FC, 1971/72 winners of the Derbyshire Senior Cup. I am in the front row, far right.

Figure 26 Buxton FC, 1972/73 Cheshire League Champions. I am in the front row, far left.

Figure 27 Manchester Evening News. February 1973

Figure 28 Mossley FC, 1976/77. I am in the back row, second from right.

Figure 29 programme for Bangor City versus Mossley,28th March 1975.

Figure 30 Team sheet for Bangor City versus Mossley, 28th March 1975.

103

CHAPTER SIX

Moving into Football Management

Mossley

I liked playing for Mossley and, as I've said, Bob trained us hard. On winter nights, he would take us to a sports hall or gym to do our training. By this time, I had started running a local open-age football team called Royston Cross, based near to my home. I gave them fitness training every week in a sports hall. I went to Bob and asked if I could do my training there instead of driving over to Mossley. Bob agreed, saying that he trusted me and knew that if I said I was training hard, I would be doing just that.

In my first season with Mossley, we won the Manchester Reporter Cup, and in 1975/76, we lost in the final of the Northern Premier League Cup. We lost to Boston United over two legs: in the first, we lost 0–4 away, and in the second, we beat them 2–1 at home. Boston's player-manager at the time was Howard Wilkinson. He played outside-right and in the two-leg final, I played left-back and had to mark him! I let him know I was there...

One of my fellow players at Mossley was called Leo Skeete. He was a centre-forward who was 6ft 2in and had part-Caribbean heritage. In the first match of the 1975/76 season, we played at Northwich Victoria, and after the match we returned to the Mossley ground. I stayed behind to have a drink with Leo. We were sitting having a beer and began discussing "coloured" people, which was the term in use at the time. I told Leo that where I came from, near Barnsley, there weren't many black or Asian people because it was a mining area. Those who had come over from other countries hadn't liked the idea of working at a 2ft 6in coal face. Many Asian people worked in the cotton mills, but there were no people of colour working down the pits. I told Leo, "You just don't see black people in Barnsley or Royston. In fact, I don't know anybody who's black."

He replied, "Well, what about me?"

One of Leo's parents was from Liverpool and the other was from the Caribbean, so he had a lighter, mixed-race skin tone. I didn't see his colour – to me he was just Leo Skeete. I said, "Well, you're not really black, are you?"

Leo replied, "Well it's funny you should say that Geoff, because on the football field nobody's ever called me a white bastard."

The 1976/77 season started poorly for Mossley and unfortunately Bob was sacked, which was a great shame. One of the club directors took charge, and he knew nothing about football. We were beaten easily in our next match. I was injured at this time,

105

having broken my toe. I volunteered to serve as acting manager until they could find someone new. I was in charge for six games, of which we won four, drew one and lost one.

The club then appointed a new manager – his name was Howard Wilkinson. It was reported that I had been overlooked for the manager's job in favour of Howard, but in reality, I didn't want the job. It wasn't in my mind at all. I knew that Howard was a real coach, but I didn't really like the idea of being coached that heavily. I knew Howard from our days in youth teams and from playing against him a few times, but really it was by reputation only. Looking back now, I think my perception of what it would be like to play for him was a bit unkind. I'd also had a bit of a sore Achilles tendon for a while, and I decided that it was time to call it a day on my career. I was 33 years old.

I played another three or four games for Mossley before I retired. Howard asked if I would stay until he found a replacement for me at left-back, and I agreed. It actually turned out that I enjoyed Howard's coaching, and I began to slightly regret my decision to retire, but Howard didn't stay long at Mossley anyway. I retired from Mossley in January 1977, and 18 months later, Howard became head of the Sheffield and Hallamshire FA. Bob Murphy then came back as manager of Mossley. On a couple of occasions when Bob had a few players out injured, he asked me to come back and play for Mossley again to help him out, which I did.

Frickley Athletic

Frickley Athletic played in the Northern Premier League. I was interviewed, alongside three other candidates, for the role of manager in November 1978. I remember the outcome of my interview well. The chairman called me into the boardroom and told me that I had been successful. He said that I would be totally in charge of running the team: that there would be no interference in football matters from the committee, but that I needed a new goalkeeper. Was that interference already, I wondered?

The club was in 22nd place in the 24-team league when I was appointed, but we managed to finish 19th at the end of the season and avoided having to apply for re-election. Before the start of the 1979/80 season, I signed several new players including Stuart Hinchcliffe, Ian Burgin, Kevin Olney, Martyn Gill, Dick Bate, David Smith, John Woodall and Dave Thompson. I had also previously signed Mick Wadsworth and Craig Smith in the 1978/79 season. Only Tommy Meehan, Keith Whiteley, Mark Jones, Nigel Long and Barry Gill remained from the players that I had inherited.

Frickley finished third in the Northern Premier League that season and were promoted to the newly formed Alliance Premier League (which is now called the National League and is the fifth tier of English football behind the Premier League, the Championship, League One and League Two). This achievement could be compared to a club such as Rochdale or Accrington Stanley playing in the Premier League nowadays.

After the first ten games or so in the Alliance Premier League, it became clear to me that we needed at least two better, more experienced players. I had already signed Gary Hooley, who later became a goalscoring success, and Mally Wright, both from lower leagues. I asked the committee for £6,000 to sign the players we needed, telling them that without it, we would more than likely face relegation back to the Northern Premier League. The committee said no, which resulted in my resignation. The following article was included in the local paper on Friday 24th October 1980:

Sleight Quits:

"The club is not geared to play at as high a standard as the Alliance Premier League."

A bombshell was dropped on the Alliance Premier League club Frickley on Monday when manager Geoff Sleight handed in his resignation. Mr Sleight told a *Times* reporter he will stay with Frickley until a new manager is appointed, providing it is not too long. He denied he was leaving to take a job with another club, although he did not rule out the possibility of continuing in management in the future. "The overriding reason why I'm leaving is because I do not think the club is geared to play at as high a standard as the Alliance Premier League," he said. "I doubt whether the area can support a team in this league, and I feel I have gone as far as I can with the club. We need two new players at the moment, but in this league, you can't just go out and pick up anybody. You must have quality players, and I cannot sign them without buying them. If I could get another couple, I believe that with the players we already have, and given a reasonable run free of injuries, we could finish in ninth or tenth position, which would be a credit to the club."

Mr Sleight emphasised that his resignation was not prompted by unpleasantness or personal feelings towards anybody. He said he had not been approached by any other club. If he were, he would consider it seriously, although he was only interested in the big clubs, not in the likes of Worksop or Goole. "Frickley went into the Alliance against my advice," he said. "I warned them of the pitfalls, because we were with the big boys now. If we want to sign a player, we have to pay for him, and also give him a higher wage than he is getting now."

Mr Sleight said the support accorded the team was disappointing, despite the fact that Frickley had one of the best records in the country by going through a season without losing on their own ground. Gates averaged only about 500 and were only slightly up this season. Several clubs in the Alliance were doubling that figure, and it meant Frickley were competing on extremely unfavourable terms.

Mr Sleight left Mossley, with whom he was playing in the Northern Premier League, to become manager of Frickley in 1978, taking over from Mr John Fairhurst. He had the satisfaction of taking Frickley into the third position of the Northern Premier League last season, a distinction which earned him promotion to the Alliance.

Frickley are advertising for a new manager immediately. Frickley's chairman, county councillor Bill Sykes, said he was disappointed to receive the resignation as Geoff had done well for the club, nobody had criticised his management, and Frickley were doing a reasonable job with their limited resources. "We have to work within our financial limitations," he said. "We're sorry we haven't the money to buy players, but who is to say that if we had more money, we should have more success? You cannot buy success, as Manchester City know."

Goole Town

After saying I wasn't interested in Worksop or Goole, in February 1981, I was approached by Goole Town to become their manager. Harry Harrison, the secretary at Goole, would not take no for an answer.

At the end of the 1980/81 season, I had taken Goole to 8th place in the Northern Premier League, which was satisfactory in the circumstances. Unfortunately, the club suffered extreme financial difficulties following discussions with the Inland Revenue, which led to them being fined £7,000. This was a tragedy because Goole Town had the nicest people imaginable on their committee and as their fans. It's probably the friendliest football club that I have ever worked with – I'm still in contact with Harry Harrison and his wife Audrey 40 years later.

Around November 1981, Frickley approached me to return. I told the new Frickley chairman, Mick Twibey, that he shouldn't be approaching me because they currently had a manager. Two days later, Mick reapproached me, saying that he had sacked the manager. I took the job at Frickley because of the ongoing financial problems at Goole.

Second Spell at Frickley Athletic

Taking the job at Frickley again was a mistake. The often used saying that you should never go back to where you have been certainly applies to my second spell at the club. I hasten to add that this was probably more to do with changes in my personal life and subsequent divorce than my relationship with the committee members. The performances of the team on the field were not what they should have been, and I was not being successful enough to put that right. When football clubs are winning, it's the players who are given the credit. When football clubs are losing, it's the manager who is held responsible. The result was that I was sacked by Mick Twibey in November 1982. I guess I took my eye off the ball!

If I was to become a manager again today, I wouldn't try to rule with an iron rod as I used to; I would do things differently. I would tell my players to play with more latitude.

The club owed me £510 in wages accumulated because of financial problems. After some discussion, I agreed to let Frickley pay me £50 a month, which they did, but for some inexplicable reason I was left £4.50 short. After my life settled down following my dismissal from Frickley, I stayed on good terms with Mick Twibey, who sadly passed away in December 2014. I still speak to his wife Pat quite often, and jokingly ask her to remind Mick when she's speaking to him "privately" about that £4.50 that technically the club still owes me. We still laugh about it.

A Fateful Football Match

The funniest and most fateful match I was ever involved with took place in March 1982, while I was working in the resources division of the education department at Barnsley Borough Council. I was in charge of the maintenance of all the schools and other educational establishment buildings within the authority and was invited to visit Lawrence Briggs Infant School at Athersley North at the request of the headteacher, Peggy Wildman. The school was in a socially deprived area of the local authority, with 100% free school meals uptake. I was to make a decision on whether to replace a long stretch of dilapidated and vandalised chain-link fencing. It was an important decision, bearing in mind that almost all of the other 120-plus schools in the local authority were in a similar position. The cost of carrying out the work required would be well beyond the amount of funding in the budget available for all aspects of maintenance work, such as roof and boiler replacements, playground resurfacing and rectifying day-to-day vandalism of the broken window kind.

Having decided that the fencing would have to wait, my conversation with the headteacher developed into one about the boys at the school, who complained that, "We never play football, because all the teachers are women and don't know how to play." Mrs Wildman was distraught that the boys were so upset, so I offered to take them for a physical education lesson in which we would play football.

There were 24 boys, so I divided them into two groups of 12 and suggested that the headteacher take one group to the local recreation area for a training run while I organised the other group to play a six-a-side game. After a 40-minute session, the two groups would swap places. It all went very well and everybody was very happy. One of the funniest occasions in the first game was when I pretended to fall over the ball to claim a foul. Three of the boys tore into me – they all started kicking me instead of the ball! It was a good lesson for me not to do that again!

In the second game, it was equally funny when one of the bigger boys, Glyn, stopped suddenly and shouted at one of the smaller boys at the top of his voice in his Barnsley accent, "Scotty, tha's got some **** on tha' boot!" Let's just say he didn't call it dog dirt! I blew the whistle to stop the game and told Glyn that he shouldn't be using swear words. He replied, "But he has! Scotty, show him that **** on tha' boot." He didn't think he was swearing, he thought that I was accusing him of telling lies! I was on educational premises, and I suppose that on this occasion I was educated by the kids from the Athersley council housing estate.

I guess that the headteacher was grateful that I had helped her and the boys. Two years later, she became Peggy Sleight, and 37 years later, she is still my wife. Thank you, Glyn and Scotty; without you and your fellow pupils, and my love for football, it would never have happened.

Royston Cross

During the period from 1970 to 1982, while I was involved with

Stalybridge Celtic, Buxton, Mossley and Frickley Athletic, I was also the chairman, manager, coach and trainer of a local football club called Royston Cross. They first approached me and asked if I would coach them, and I was able to improve their performances considerably. I ran the club from top to bottom, doing everything.

The club played in the Barnsley League – on Saturdays at first, and on Sundays later on. It grew in strength and was very successful over the 12 years I spent there, winning many trophies, including the Royston Charity Cup in 1974 and 1982, and the Beckett Cup at Oakwell. They also secured promotion through the league system from the Nelson League to the Barnsley Premier League.

There were at least eight or nine players I had at Royston Cross to whom I gave a chance to kick on and play at a higher level at Mossley or Frickley. However, as good as they were as players, they just didn't have the temperament to get out of their comfort zones and compete against better players.

The club and players couldn't have achieved such success without the contribution of the committee members, who worked tirelessly to raise funds so that players didn't have to pay annual subscriptions, to buy new strips regularly, and to contribute to local charity organisations in the village. The committee members, who all deserve recognition, were Stan Hutchinson, Billy Horner, Brian Wilson, Rhys Williams, David

Woolhouse, Keith Nixon, Jeff Hay and Mick Proctor. They were brilliant. I would invite them to my house for dinner and we would have a five-hour meeting to talk about what the club needed. They were so good at then going off and raising the money.

Figure 31Frickley Athletic 1979/80 manager of the month. I am holding the bottle.

Figure 32 Frickley Athletic 1979/80. I am in the front row, far left.

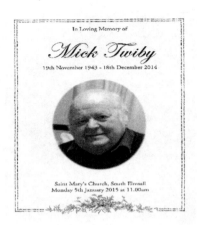

Figure 33 Funeral service for Mick Twiby, chairman of Frickley Athletic, 5th January 2015.

Figure 34 Royston Cross presentation evening. I am receiving an award from Francis Lee, 1977.

Figure 35 Royston Cross FC presentation evening. I am receiving an award from John Charles, 1978.

Figure 36 Royston Cross FC presentation evening. I am receiving an award from Alan Clarke, manager at Barnsley FC, 1979.

CHAPTER SEVEN

Scouting for Leeds United

In October 1988, Howard Wilkinson left Sheffield Wednesday to become manager of Leeds United, along with his assistant manager, Mick Hennigan. I had been out of football completely since I'd finished at Frickley in 1982. I called Howard to wish him and Mick all the best at Leeds United, and he invited me to the ground at Elland Road to see him. He asked me, "Would you do some part-time scouting for players until I appoint a chief scout? I want you to look for young players or professionals."

I told him, "I'd be happy to help you out in the short-term, but I don't know anything about scouting kids."

We agreed that I would scout for professional players. When Ian MacFarlane was appointed as chief scout shortly after this, I continued scouting players until the end of the 1988/89 season, when Leeds United finished in a respectable mid-table position in the Second Division (now called the Championship).

At the beginning of the 1989/90 season, Ian MacFarlane told me, totally unexpectedly, that the gaffer wanted me to do a match report on the Middlesbrough versus Wolverhampton Wanderers game, as Leeds were due to play Middlesbrough at home on the following Monday evening. I had never done a match report in my life, and I didn't have any idea how to do one. I went to the game, which Middlesbrough won 4–2, while Leeds United were being beaten 2–5 at Newcastle. I then wrote what I perceived to be a match report on Middlesbrough. The following Monday, the Middlesbrough right full-back scored an own goal in the 89th minute to give Leeds a 2–1 victory, and it was all due to the match report...that was my reasoning, anyway! Without any comment from anybody, I continued doing match reports as well as scouting players throughout my career at Leeds United.

A good example of the value of match reports came a few years later, when Bryn Law, a local journalist, asked me what I knew about AS Monaco. Leeds were due to play Monaco in the first round of the UEFA Cup in 1995, and I'd watched Monaco three times. I gave Bryn a copy of my match report in answer to his question. Leeds United won the match 3–0, with Tony Yeboah scoring a hat-trick. Bryn later told me that he had never understood a match so clearly as he did that night, due to my match report. It seems that my report changed his way of watching and understanding football. Bryn went on to work for Sky, and appears to still be enjoying a successful career in the media.

The match reports that I produced for Howard didn't change much over the years that I wrote them. Each report would take me about 2 hours and 45 minutes to do. You start off with the teams, then talk about their shape, the individual players and their strengths and weaknesses. Then, you talk about the set plays; the free kicks for and against. They were very detailed. Howard never gave me any feedback, and that's as big a compliment as you could get from Howard. That's just how he was, and I mean that respectfully. There are many more things that I like about Howard than those things which I don't like. If I had to give him a middle name, I'd call him Howard "Thorough" Wilkinson.

Howard is also the person with the greatest understanding of fitness that I have ever known. He was way ahead of his time in terms of measuring training and deciding just how much to do for the players at any given time. Howard used a lot of clichés, but clichés are informative because they're usually valid. He would always say, "Fail to prepare, and be prepared to fail." He also said, "Practice doesn't make perfect, perfect practice makes perfect." That would never have been thought of when I was a youngster, but it's the sort of word-usage that you tend to hear nowadays. It has to be the right kind of practice to get the result you want.

Howard told me once that he employed me at Leeds United because I had an opinion which was not necessarily the same as his – I was not a yes man. I've got the utmost respect for Howard Wilkinson, but I would say that while I did learn a lot from him, he never taught me anything directly. I watched him and I listened to him and as a result

I learnt, but I had to work it out myself – he didn't share his thoughts. The most important aspect of scouting players that I deduced without being told was to focus on the player, not the game. It was also important to make a decision after watching a player for the first time, but to be prepared to change my mind when watching them for the second time. Doing so might suggest having been wrong in the first place, but we all have good days and bad days. When you're contemplating buying a player for millions of pounds, it's essential that every aspect of his game is recognised and understood. I worked that out after assessing Howard's approach and attitude. He never actually told me.

In the last match of the 1989/90 season, Leeds secured a 1–0 victory at Bournemouth while our closest rivals, Newcastle United, were beaten 1–4 at Middlesbrough. Consequently, Leeds United were promoted as champions to the First Division (not yet called the Premier League). The following season, 1990/91, Leeds finished in fourth place in the First Division, but in the following 1991/92 season, they went on to win the First Division title. The memories of such a momentous occasion have probably been brought into perspective by the fact that Leeds United have not been within touching distance of repeating this achievement during the following 29 years, at the time of writing.

Despite starting the 1992/93 season as champions, Leeds suffered something of a reversal of fortunes. They were knocked out of what is now the Champions League by Rangers and finished 17th in the newly-named Premier League. This contrasted with the fact that their home form was among the best in the Premier League. They lost only once at Elland Road, when they were beaten 1–4 by a Nottingham Forest team who had managed to score five goals against both Blackburn Rovers and Tottenham Hotspur earlier in the season (both of whom finished in the top eight). However, a failure to win away from home all season cost Leeds dearly. As the season drew to a close, they were in danger of being only the second team in history to be relegated the season after winning the title. They managed to secure safety with a few matches to spare, although they did finish only two points away from relegation. Crystal Palace, Middlesbrough and Nottingham Forest were the teams actually relegated that year.

Early in December 1993, the chief scout, Ian MacFarlane, was taken ill. I offered to do the job for Howard temporarily until Ian recovered. In January 1994, indications were that Ian would not recover sufficiently to carry out a job which was particularly stressful. I was offered the post of chief scout on a full-time basis, to be effective from 1st February 1994. Initially, I turned the job down, because I had 27 years of service in local government and needed 40 years to qualify for a full retirement pension. I offered to carry on until the end of the season, or until Howard could find a new chief scout. Howard agreed. I then began negotiations with Barnsley Council, who were actually seeking candidates for early retirement due to a downturn in local government expenditure across the board. I managed to obtain early retirement, which took effect from 30th April 1994, and signed a five-year contract with Leeds United which took effect from 1st May 1994.

My first overseas trip as chief scout was to watch Estonia lose 0–2 to Wales in Tallinn. I went especially to watch Mart Poom, the Estonian goalkeeper. Poom did enough for me to be interested, but not enough to recommend him at this stage, although he did go on to play over 200 games in England, mainly at Derby Country, Sunderland and Watford, and 120 internationals for his country.

The morning after the game, I was getting ready to go home when there was a knock on my hotel room door. When I answered, there were five policemen standing there with dogs. They said that they were looking for drugs. For a split second, I was scared, very scared. I had images in my head of me vanishing into Russia! I was so relieved when they then said, "Sorry, we've got the wrong room." I went downstairs in a big hurry to where the Welsh team were waiting for their coach to take them to the airport. I met the manager, Mike Smith, and the coach, Dave Williams (who in 1995 came to coach at Leeds and is a good friend of mine). I welcomed their invitation of a lift to the airport in the Welsh team coach.

Around this time, at the end of the 1993/94 season, Howard Wilkinson received a video from John Brooks, a contact he had in South Africa, which showed a 2–2 draw between Zambia and South Africa. It was accompanied by a strong recommendation for Lucas Radebe, a central defender for Kaizer Chiefs. Having watched the video, I suggested that I go over to Johannesburg and watch a friendly game between Kaizer Chiefs and Liverpool.

The game was being played on a Sunday. As I arrived at my hotel around Saturday lunchtime, I was met by an agent who wanted to take me, Bob Houghton (the Zurich coach) and Bobby Robson (then manager of Porto) to watch a right full-back and a midfield player who were playing for Mamelodi Sundowns against Wits University. Having flown for ten hours through the night and then having gone straight to a football match, I was very tired and not very excited by the performance of the two players we had been brought to watch. However, the big centre-forward playing for Mamelodi caught my attention – enough for me to make a note to check him out on the video of the Zambia versus South Africa game when I got home. His name was Philemon Masinga.

The following day, we were in the guest box at the Kaizer Chiefs versus Liverpool game. As we stood for the national

126

anthems to be played, I realised that Lucas Radebe wasn't playing. I said to Bob Houghton, "The player we've come here to watch isn't playing," to which Bob retorted, "You don't know who I've come to watch." I responded, "Bob, I know who we've both come to watch." Lucas had turned his ankle in training the previous day and was not fit enough to play in the game.

The game ended in a 0–0 draw, but the party wasn't over yet. Back at the hotel, some of the Kaizer Chiefs players came into the bar where we were having a drink. One of them was Steve Komphela, the South African captain. The players didn't know who I was, but I chatted to them, suggesting that a 0–0 draw with Liverpool was a good result for the Kaizer Chiefs.

"It was," Steve Komphela agreed, "but it might've been better if we'd fielded a full team."

I knew exactly what he meant, but I asked him, "Who wasn't playing?"

"Lucas Radebe. He injured his ankle in training yesterday."

"Is Lucas a good player?" I asked.

Steve said, quite emphatically, "He's the best player in South Africa."

Fortunately, my journey didn't turn out to be a waste of time because when I got home the following day, I checked the video again, and Masinga did enough for me to watch him play again. By coincidence, South Africa were going to Australia a few days later to play two games against the Socceroos in Adelaide and Sydney. Howard was away on holiday, so I suggested to Bill Fotherby, the managing director, that I go to the two games. He agreed, but stressed that I shouldn't travel business class!

When I arrived in Adelaide, I checked in at the Hilton Hotel and then went to find the hotel where the South African team were staying. It didn't take long before I located it, and I casually walked into the lounge where the South Africans were sitting. I talked in general terms to the team's coach about the two games against Australia, without letting him know who I was. The information I was looking for was whether or not he had a full team. The answer was no, because Lucas Radebe had turned an ankle the previous week (which I already knew) and hadn't travelled. Not what I was hoping to hear, but I decided that I would stay for the two games, concentrate on watching Masinga, and then see some friends in Sydney.

Masinga did well enough in both games, and I spoke to him afterwards to ask whether he would like to come to Leeds United. He said that Porto and Zurich had already expressed an interest, so I told him that I would speak to the owner of Mamelodi Sundowns when I got home and Leeds would make an offer. The Sundowns accepted an offer of £275,000 and we made arrangements for Masinga to come to Leeds – which didn't happen without incident.

I received a telephone call from a customs officer at Heathrow Airport asking if I knew a football player called Philemon Masinga. When Philemon had been asked where he was going by the customs officer, he had panicked at being confronted by what he considered to be white officialdom. Relationships between white people and black people in South Africa at the time were improving rapidly because of the statesmanship of Nelson Mandela, but they were not 100% proven in the eyes of some black people. Philemon had thought that he wouldn't be believed if he said that he was going to play for Leeds United, so he'd told them that he was going to Leeds to see a girlfriend. Apparently, this wasn't a strong enough reason for him to be granted entry to the country. I told the customs officer that I did know Philemon and that I was expecting him at Leeds United anytime soon. The situation was sorted out, but it wasn't the best of starts for Philemon!

Having signed Masinga, Howard then asked me what we should do about Lucas Radebe, having not actually seen him play. Appreciating what Howard was saying, I told him everything that I had learnt about Radebe as a player from his contemporaries. "If we don't sign him," I said, "someone else will." We brought Lucas over for the 1994/95 pre-season friendly matches in Europe, where he did enough in the

129

circumstances for Howard to buy him for £250,000.

Some information that appeared in the media in relation to Lucas Radebe's career at Leeds United is untrue. Contrary to reports that Lucas was only signed to be company for Philemon Masinga, Lucas was in fact the original target. It was also reported that both Lucas and Philemon were recommended by Howard's contact in South Africa. As the one person who was most involved in signing the players, I can confirm that neither Howard nor myself had heard of Philemon Masinga until I went to the Mamelodi Sundowns game against Wits University.

Unfortunately, Philemon didn't play enough games in his first season to justify a work permit for a second season. Instead, he moved to St Gallen in Switzerland, and then to Salernitana and Bari in the Italian Serie A, where he did well. Sadly, Philemon passed away in 2019 at the age of 49.

One nice memory about Philemon is that when his first daughter was born in 1995, my wife Peggy and myself bought a large cuddly teddy bear for her. When I gave it to Philemon in the carpark at Elland Road, he looked around to see if anybody was watching and then asked me if I would take it to his car for him! He felt that it would be very embarrassing if anybody saw him carrying a teddy bear. He was 6ft 4in and couldn't be seen carrying a teddy bear – but surely that couldn't be worse than being kicked all round a football pitch by Tony Adams when he played against Arsenal! However, it was very reminiscent of the story of me carrying anniversary flowers for Nat Lofthouse while at Bolton Wanderers way back in 1962! It must be something to do with that number nine shirt.

Lucas Radebe, meanwhile, became a legend, and is still regarded as such by Leeds United supporters. He retired in 2005. I'm still in touch with Lucas, but more so with his former partner Tumi and his daughter Jesse.

There were several other important signings that I was involved in at Leeds, including Nigel Martyn. Players reaching the age of 35 were able to leave their clubs on a free transfer. Towards the end of the 1995/96 season, indications were that goalkeeper John Lukic would be leaving Leeds to return to his former club, Arsenal, under this new ruling. Howard asked me quite bluntly one day if I'd signed a goalkeeper for him to replace John Lukic. He knew the answer really, as he was the one who actually signed the players. I told him that the two best goalkeepers at the time were David Seaman at Arsenal and Tim Flowers at Blackburn Rovers, but that neither were available. The only two reasonable possibilities were Alan Kelly at Sheffield United and Nigel Martyn at Crystal Palace.

"Kelly has a bad back, so we can forget him," Howard said.

"That only leaves Nigel Martyn," I replied.

"But he's going to Everton for £1.75 million," said Howard.

131

"What d'you think I should do?"

I thought that Howard was in an indifferent mood at the time, so I suggested, "Call Ron Noades (the Crystal Palace chairman) and find out how far negotiations have gone for the transfer. If it hasn't been completed yet, I think you should offer £2 million for Nigel Martyn."

Surprisingly, Howard rang Ron Noades immediately and learnt that the transfer was to be carried out the following day. It had been delayed because Joe Royle, the Everton manager, was not available to complete the transaction at the time. Howard offered £2.25 million for the goalkeeper. The next day, Joe Royle was still not available, but the club secretary was expected to complete the signing which all seemed cut and dried. Nigel Martyn's adviser then told Everton that the player wouldn't be signing immediately, as he had another interested club to speak to before making a decision. Arrangements were made immediately for Nigel and his family to come to a hotel in Harrogate. I looked after Nigel's wife and son while he met with Howard and Bill Fotherby. Howard and Bill took Nigel on a tour around Elland Road and the club's new training facilities at Thorpe Arch. Negotiations were successful, and Nigel Martyn signed for Leeds United.

While he was at Leeds, Nigel was named officially as the club's greatest ever goalkeeper, beating off competition from the likes of Gary Sprake, David Harvey and John Lukic. Ironically,

Nigel later signed for Everton in 2003, following a disagreement with the Leeds manager, Terry Venables. Nigel is fondly remembered in Leeds as not only a great goalkeeper, but also for the way he and his wife supported parents who suffered the trauma of miscarriage.

Martyn Gill, who was scouting for me in the south, had watched Lee Bowyer several times and then recommended that we sign him. I watched him three times, and I was convinced that Lee was as good a player as Martyn had reported. Howard watched him once, and agreed to the extent that he signed Lee during the close season of 1996 for £2.5 million, making him the most expensive teenager ever at the time.

Howard had arranged a pre-season trip to Europe in July 1996. At the time of departure from Elland Road, Howard received a call from Lee Bowyer to say that he was lost in the middle of a roundabout in the city! Howard asked me to go and find him before the coach set off for Manchester Airport. I established that Lee was in the carpark of the Asda offices in the middle of the Crown Point roundabout, which had five exit points. He had driven round the roundabout six times without recognising which was the exit to Elland Road! I found Lee ten minutes later as he was being confronted by the manager of the Asda offices, who was threatening to report him to the police for parking there. I quickly explained the situation to the office manager and took Lee to catch the coach at Elland Road. However, the coach had already left for Manchester, so I then had to drive him to the airport. Although I'd been involved in signing Lee a couple of weeks earlier, he didn't have any idea who I was and offered me £10 for "saving" him. I told him that wasn't necessary!

Lee was a skilful, hard-running midfielder who didn't mind a tackle. He scored on his debut against Derby County in the first match of the season.

I had learnt over the past couple of years that working as chief scout for Howard Wilkinson involved more than just watching football matches. For example, when Gary McAllister played for Scotland in Glasgow, and Gary Speed played for Wales in Cardiff, Howard didn't like the idea of players driving for long distances back to Leeds having just played a game. Nor did he want them staying overnight and then driving home the day after, instead of spending the day recuperating. He made it my job to make sure that after the matches, they got home the same night. So, I went to Glasgow on three occasions to watch Gary McAllister play against San Marino, Australia and Greece at Hampden Park. On another occasion, I picked him up at Glasgow Airport after he played in Moscow. I actually listened to the Scotland versus Russia game on the car radio while driving up to Glasgow and arrived at the same time as Gary's plane arrived from Moscow. On all four occasions, I dropped

Gary off at home in Boston Spa and didn't arrive back at my own home until around 5am.

In November 1994, I picked up Gary Speed from Cardiff after Wales had just lost 0–3 to Bulgaria. Paul Hart, who was in charge of the academy at the time, had to drive me to Cardiff because Gary, often referred to as "Speedo", had driven himself down but was not allowed to drive himself back. After the match, Paul drove me to the hotel where Gary was staying and set off home. An hour later, once Speedo had showered and come to the hotel, he wanted to stay for a drink. I refused and asked him where his car was. "This is it," he said, as we approached a brand new, black £60,000 Porsche sportscar which he'd paid for with money he'd recently earnt doing some male modelling. I didn't want to drive the car, and Gary didn't want me to drive it either! I agreed that Gary could drive us home, so long as he didn't tell Howard!

Howard didn't approve of the staff at Elland Road associating with players in their private lives. However, in 1995, my wife and I met some friends from America on the beautiful Caribbean island of Grand Cayman. By sheer coincidence, Speedo and his lovely fiancée, Louise, were in the same hotel. We got together to enjoy a fantastic week with Gary, Louise and our friends from America.

While I was at Leeds and making overseas trips to watch

135

players, Louise would often come to our home in Woolley to spend a day with Peggy. We were even invited to their wedding, which was on the May bank holiday weekend in 1996.

Sadly, Speedo passed away in tragic circumstances in 2011. A short time afterwards, I spoke to Howard as he was driving home from Speedo's funeral service in Chester. I confessed that I hadn't driven Speedo back from Cardiff that night, 17 years earlier. Howard was not amused.

The popularity of Gary Speed as a person and a player is detailed in depth in a book titled *Gary Speed. Unspoken: The Family's Untold Story.* He will always be a part of Leeds United's history. Rest in peace Speedo.

During the 1995/96 season, Harry Kewell became eligible to sign as a full-time professional. Harry's parents, Rod and Helen, came over from Australia for this occasion. As often happened in such a situation, Howard asked me to look after Rod and Helen while he spoke to Bill Fotherby and Harry. As I'd lived in Australia in the 1960s, I had plenty to talk about with Rod and Helen; the conversation was very enlightening. Rod told me that he actually came from Wales, but had "jumped ship" in Australia in 1967 while he was working in the Merchant Navy. He said that this was the first time he had been out of Australia since then. I found that quite surprising and very interesting. Having both a British passport and an Australian passport myself, I use my Australian passport to enter Australia, which means that I don't need a visa. Rod said that he didn't have an Australian passport, so had left Sydney on his British passport and hadn't had a problem getting out of Australia or into the UK. I then asked him, "But how are you going to get back into Australia without a visa?"

He replied, "I've lived in Australia for 28 years. I'm married to an Australian girl, and all my children are Australian."

"But that's all irrelevant," I explained. "You'll have problems getting back through customs without a visa – you'll be regarded as a foreigner."

Fortunately, the Australian Embassy had an office in Manchester at the time. I called them and explained Rod's position, asking for advice on how to deal with it. I was told to take Rod and Helen to Manchester straight away. My interpretation was correct: Rod would not have been allowed back into Australia under his given circumstances alone. The Australian Embassy were helpful in the extreme, and did what was necessary to allow Rod Kewell back into Australia, although they did confirm that he wouldn't have been, had I not acted so quickly!

I haven't seen Harry Kewell since, and on the occasions that I have tried to contact Rod and Helen when I've been in Australia, I've not been able to do so. Their son Harry was a brilliant player at Leeds United, as he was at Liverpool, although he did suffer a lot of injuries at Anfield which prevented him from reaching his full potential. I think he was badly advised to sign for Galatasaray, taking into consideration the deaths of two Leeds United fans which had occurred during riots when Leeds were playing in the UEFA Cup semi-final in Istanbul. I think that Harry had the potential to become one of Leeds United's greatest players. As a Socceroo, I am of the opinion that Harry Kewell is Australia's greatest ever player.

The number of football agents increased rapidly from 1995 onwards, following the freedom of contract permitted as a result of the Bosman Ruling by the European Court of Justice. Probably the most well-known agent at the time was Rune Hauge, who made headlines when he was banned for life for being embroiled in an allegation of paying George Graham a £425,000 bung to sign players. The ban was reduced to two years on appeal. Graham was later found guilty by the Football Association for receiving an "unsolicited gift" and suspended for two years. This was reduced to one year on appeal by the League Managers Association. Ironically, this was chaired by Howard Wilkinson, who was later sacked by Leeds United and replaced by George Graham.

In October 1995, Rune Hauge invited me and representatives of six other English clubs (including Les Kershaw of Manchester

United and Bruce Rioch of Arsenal), to two games. The first was in Stavanger on 10th October, and the second in Oslo on 11th October. The first match was a 2–2 draw between Norway under-23s and England under-23s. The second match was a 0–0 draw between the two countries' senior international teams. After the first game, we all attended dinner at the hotel where Bruce Rioch and myself discussed Elvis Presley while the others discussed the game! (My three heroes, in order of preference, are Elvis Presley, Serena Williams and Tiger Woods. Elvis was the greatest singer and entertainer there has ever been and ever will be; Serena Williams is the greatest female tennis player there has ever been; and Tiger Woods is the greatest golfer there's ever been. In my opinion, anyway.)

When we were leaving for Oslo the following morning, we were settling payment for the hotel rooms when Les Kershaw asked me how much my room had cost. I told him I had paid £95. Les showed me his room, which was a posh suite costing him £325! Les said that Rune had put him in that particular room as a joke because Les worked for Manchester United and Rune thought that the club could afford it. We all saw the funny side, which was more than we could say about the 0–0 draw between Norway and England that night in Oslo.

Before we'd signed Nigel Martyn, I had been to look at a goalkeeper and a left-back at Sparta Prague. I'd thought that neither of the players would enhance the squad at Leeds, but the one player who did impress me was an attacking midfielder called Pavel Nedvěd. It had been an afternoon game, which allowed myself and the agent I was with to call in at the square in the middle of Prague (a lovely place) that evening for a drink with a couple of the players, one of whom happened to be Pavel Nedvěd. I wasn't interested in the player being promoted to me by the agent, but I asked Pavel if he fancied coming to Leeds United, to which he said yes. I reported to Howard that the goalkeeper and left-back were not what we wanted, but that I'd seen a very good attacking midfield player. Howard's reaction was that he wanted a goalkeeper and a left-back, not a midfielder.

Pavel Nedvěd went on to win the Player of The Year award in Italy, and became recognised as the best player in Europe for a time. When I reminded Howard of this missed opportunity several years later, he suggested that everybody in football has that type of story to tell! In 1996, Pavel featured in the very strong Czech Republic team who progressed to the final of the Euro 1996 tournament before losing 1–2 to Germany at Wembley. Two of the players from that Czech squad who impressed me were Karel Poborský and Patrik Berger (who went to Manchester United and Liverpool respectively).

Another occasion when Howard asked me to entertain someone while he was with the chairman was when Graeme

140

Souness came to see him. It was at the time when Graeme was the manager of Rangers in Glasgow, and was recovering from heart surgery. When I asked him what he was doing while he was convalescing, Graeme said, "You won't believe me, but I enjoy spending time in the garden by myself, pruning the roses."

Knowing that he was probably the hardest player that I'd ever seen, I asked, "How do you do that, by biting their heads off?"

I think about that day every time I see Graeme on TV as a pundit, where he is, in my opinion, the best of them all.

Quite often, I found myself entertaining people at Elland Road by default. Frequently, I saw John Charles wander into the car park. He had fallen on bad times financially in his later life, and it was such a shame that a player widely believed to be Leeds United's greatest ever should find himself in such a predicament. Whatever I was doing, when I saw John, I would stop and take him into the canteen for a cup of tea. I would then sit and listen to his stories about when he was at Leeds United and Juventus in the 1950s. If my memory serves me well, he was sold to Juventus in 1957 for a record £65,000, and there won the Serie A three times and the Coppa Italia twice. It was an honour to meet and listen to the football memories of a Yorkshire Welshman!

The year before I started scouting for Leeds, my wife Peggy was appointed as an education adviser at Leeds City Council.

From 1990 onwards, as part of her work, she set up a study support centre under the South Stand at Elland Road. Primary school children from across the local authority made one day visits to Elland Road to study the national curriculum, using the football club as an educational resource. Football was used as a way of engaging the children with a range of subjects. These included Mathematics (numbers, shapes, space, measurement and handling data), English (development of speaking, listening and reporting skills), Science (nutrition, movement and growth), History (understanding reasons for change and interpreting the past), Geography (distances travelled to different countries where football is played), Design Technology (making structures), IT (analysing information used to control crowds), Art (drawing, painting and experimenting with kit design), Music (looking at the melody and lyrics of football songs, and how sound created atmosphere), Physical Education (understanding movement in the game), and Religious Education (to pray that their team won). Not really – I made that last one up!

On these visits, opportunities arose for the children to listen to a guest speaker. This would usually be a player, but when the players were unavailable, I often stepped in to talk to the students, relating my scouting role and experiences. This was not a duty featured in any typical chief scout job description, but when Peggy and Howard are either side of you, anything goes!

I'm friendly with a couple of lovely people who have been among the top echelon of Leeds United supporters all their lives. I first met Phil Beeton when I was watching the Leeds reserve team play in the first week after I had agreed to do some scouting for Howard. Phil and his wife, Christine (known as Chris), have watched Leeds United play on more than 2,300 occasions, home and away, and we have kept in touch with each other since I left Leeds in 1996. Our friendship was strengthened even more when Ken Bates became the owner of the club and banned all the players from having any association at all with the supporters. This included banning players from attending the supporters' club annual dinner and dance, an occasion which allowed supporters to meet and talk to their idols face to face, something which all football fans want to do. In order to enable the annual dinner and dance to survive, the committee decided to invite ex-players and club personalities to attend the function instead. I was flattered to be considered an ex-Leeds United personality and, thanks to Phil and Chris, Peggy and I were invited several times alongside others including Lucas Radebe, Gary Kelly, Neil Aspin, Noel Whelan, Andy Ritchie and Kevin Sharp.

Perhaps I was first invited because Phil remembered that when I was chief scout, he had asked me to speak to his branch of the supporters' club at The Golden Lion in the city centre.

I suggested to Phil that rather than speak for an hour, I would tell them what my job involved for 15 minutes or so and then take questions from the fans, staying for as long as it took to answer them. Phil thought that was a good idea, and things got even better for the supporters when Lucas Radebe, who was staying at The Golden Lion at the time, turned up to join the party!

The Q&A went well, and by the end, Phil was very pleased with what he thought was a successful meeting. The supporters had asked a wide range of questions, the first of which had been, "When is Maradona coming?" Apparently, it had been in *The Yorkshire Post* or *The Evening News* that Bill Fotherby had said that the club was signing Diego Maradona for the forthcoming season. Maradona and Pelé are considered to be the two greatest football players of all time. I asked the supporter what time of year it was. When he replied that it was July, I asked him when season tickets went on sale for the upcoming season. He replied that it would be later that month. I then told him that I wasn't aware that Maradona was coming to Leeds United, but that maybe the managing director was attempting to use a clever sales ploy to boost the sale of season tickets. There was never any evidence that Maradona was going to arrive at Elland Road! My opinion is that 50% of what is written in the sports pages is true, and the other 50% is false. The problem is that it's not easy to recognise which is which, and people tend to believe what they want to be true.

The 1995/96 season was a relatively disappointing one. Leeds United finished 13th in the Premier League, and though they did reach the final of the League Cup at Wembley, they lost 0–3 to Aston Villa. The club made a respectable start to the 1996/97 season: they were in ninth position, earning seven points from their first four games, when they were heavily beaten 0–4 at home by Manchester United on 7th September.

Howard Wilkinson, Mick Hennigan and Eddie Gray were sacked by Caspian, the new owners of the club, on 9th September. Eddie Gray was subsequently reinstated. At the time, I was due to go to Colombia to watch a couple of players. It was a trip that I wasn't looking forward to at all because of the problems in the country related to drug trafficking. I decided to stay quiet about the planned trip and never went! Every cloud has a silver lining – at least it did for me on this occasion.

I was sacked on 7th November 1996 by Howard's replacement as manager, George Graham. When I asked if my dismissal was anything to do with my ability or inability to do the job, George Graham said that I was still considered to be one of Howard's staff. I considered that to be a compliment.

I had two and a half years of my contract with Leeds United left to run. The following 18 months of my football life were spent in a legal battle with the club, as my extremely well-paid solicitor and I fought for me to be adequately compensated.

We eventually succeeded. Howard Wilkinson actually facilitated the end of the protracted negotiations through a conversation he had with Jeremy Fenn, a director of Caspian, about the FA's provision of tickets for the Italy versus England World Cup qualifier of the previous year. Howard was now working for the FA, and the outcome of his conversation with Jeremy Fenn was that Jeremy now felt he owed Howard a favour because of the way he'd arranged for Howard to provide him with tickets. Howard suggested that my contract wrangle should be resolved. Two days later, everything was sorted out.

I was with Leeds United for eight years, working part-time for the first five while I continued my employment with Barnsley Council, and then spending three years with the club full-time as chief scout. During that time, I travelled across 20 different countries: England, Northern Ireland, Scotland, Wales, Ireland, Sweden, Denmark, Norway, Estonia, Belgium, Holland, France, Germany, Spain, Portugal, Switzerland, Poland, the Czech Republic, South Africa and Australia. Usually, I was heading to a country either to watch a specific player, or to produce a match report on an upcoming opponent. Despite an unpleasant end to my career at Leeds United, it was a pleasure to work for Howard Wilkinson, and a pleasure to work for the club.

Figure 37 Appointed chief scout at Leeds United, 1st May 1994.

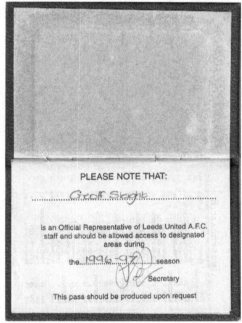

Figure 38 Chief scout identification pass for Leeds United, 1996/97.

Figure 39 Having a beer with Gary Speed in Grand Cayman, 1995.

Figure 40 Louise, Gary Speed, Peggy, me, Ron and Alison in Grand Cayman, 1995.

148

Figure 41 Dining out in Grand Cayman with Louise, Speedo, Ron and Alison in 1995.

CHAPTER EIGHT

Post-1996: The Later Years

In January 1997, four months after leaving Leeds United, Howard Wilkinson was hired by the Football Association (FA) to act as Technical Director overseeing coaching. He worked on the promotion and formation of the academy system, initially at Premier League clubs, and under him the FA began the National Football Centre in the Midlands. I travelled with Howard on visits to all the Premier League clubs in the country, and even to Paris to meet with Gérard Houllier. Gérard was in a similar position at the French Football Association and later became a successful manager at Liverpool. I assisted Howard by writing the minutes of all the meetings and sending them to his secretary at the FA so that he could concentrate on the discussions taking place. It was a very pleasant surprise when the FA paid me expenses for my time and contribution, allowing me to take Peggy to Barbados for a couple of weeks – an unexpected but very enjoyable conclusion.

In many ways, my involvement in football from the inside was over at this period – so much so that when Howard resigned as Technical Director at the FA in 2002 and became the manager of Sunderland, I secretly hoped that he wouldn't ask me to get involved again up on Wearside.

Fortunately, and unexpectedly, my time was taken up by a visit from the members of the North Korean team that had shocked the world in the 1966 World Cup by beating Italy 1–0 in the group stages at Middlesbrough. They went on to lead Portugal 3–0 after 20 minutes in the quarter-final game at Everton's Goodison Park, before Eusebio scored four goals in an eventual 5–3 victory. Eusebio's performance enabled Portugal to avoid being the second major victim of the North Korean team who had thwarted my own ambitions to play for Australia in the 1966 World Cup Finals.

Everton marked their centenary year in 2002. As part of the celebrations, an invitation was issued to the North Korean government for their 1966 team to visit Everton in October. The visit would also allow the team members to travel to Ayresome Park in Middlesbrough and relive their momentous victory over Italy. In October 2001, after four years of negotiations with Daniel Gordon, the owner of a Sheffield company called Very Much So Productions, unprecedented access to North Korea was granted and he set about finding the surviving members of the heroic 1966 team in order to tell their story. The result was an 80-minute documentary called *The Game of Their Lives* which was first broadcast by the BBC shortly before the start of the World Cup in May 2002. It was later shown in its entirety in both North and South Korea. The film was made in association with Passion Pictures and the

BBC. It was intended that the film would be officially premiered at the Sheffield Film Festival during the North Korean team's visit.

When Daniel Gordon was told by Howard Wilkinson that I'd played for Australia against North Korea in the World Cup qualifier in 1965, and now lived in Wakefield, Daniel asked if he could interview me to gather my comments on the North Koreans who were the subject of his film. As a result of that interview, Dave Todd (who was living in Liverpool) and myself were invited to Goodison Park to attend the forthcoming game between Everton and Arsenal. Incidentally, that game was the debut of a 17-year-old called Wayne Rooney who came on as a substitute in the second half and scored a tremendous goal, giving Everton a 2–1 victory. It was Wayne Rooney's first step towards becoming a football legend for Manchester United and an England all time great.

The day after the match at Goodison, while preparing to attend a visit to a stately home in Derbyshire with the North Korean party, I narrowly avoided a diplomatic disaster. When I was at Leeds United, I had acquired a Puma trainer's coat which I had never worn because it was too big for me. I had also acquired a Premier League tie when I'd been accompanying Howard Wilkinson, also never worn. I thought that it would be a friendly gesture to give the coat to Rim Yung Son, who I'd played against directly in Cambodia, and the tie to

Han Bong Jin, the flying winger who had caused us the most damage in that 1–6 defeat. I got the Puma coat out of the wardrobe to check that it was alright and noticed on the label that it had been "Made in South Korea". Phew! That was a close call! Peggy unpicked the label and took it out, thus avoiding what might have caused some embarrassment. The visit was enjoyable, even though I could only speak to the players through an interpreter.

A day or two later, Peggy and myself attended the film premier of *The Game of Their Lives* at Sheffield. Afterwards, we were invited to the Holiday Inn where the North Koreans were staying before moving on to Middlesbrough. We spent a pleasant hour or so talking to the players, ensuring that the interpreters could justify their presence. Apparently, because the film was being shown daily on the state-operated television channel in North Korea, I was recognised and well-known there! I was invited, through the interpreter, to visit Pyongyang. It was a visit which never materialised. I wasn't able to accompany the North Koreans and their party to Middlesbrough because two days later I was going to Australia, of all places, for the imminent Ashes series.

When I returned from Australia, Daniel Gordon asked if I would write a letter to Pyongyang to tell them how much I'd enjoyed meeting the North Koreans. I received a reply written in beautiful Korean handwriting that needed to be translated by a contact of Daniel's from Sheffield University. I had addressed my letter to "my dear friends in North Korea" and concluded by saying that although our governments had different views, we shared a strong friendship through football. Shortly afterwards, I discovered that my letter had appeared on the internet. Earlier in the year, the incoming US President, George W Bush, in his first State of the Union address, had described Iraq, Iran and North Korea as "an axis of evil". For days afterwards, I was expecting our house to be wiped off the face of the earth by some missile from the USA! Or at least to be recognised by customs officers when entering the USA on holiday!

In 2003, *The Game of Their Lives* won the Royal Television Society's award for the Best Sports Documentary of the year. Meeting the North Korean party was one of the highlights of my football memories, and of my life.

My next involvement in football was in 2005. Australia were playing Uruguay in the final qualifiers for the World Cup due to be held in Germany in 2006. Having lost 0–1 in Uruguay, the Socceroos had given themselves the opportunity to win the tie on aggregate in the return game in Sydney on 16th November. The Football Federation of Australia invited the 1965 squad to the game and provided us with complimentary tickets at a reunion meal in the city. In a nail-biting 1–0 victory to Australia, after extra-time, "we" won the game in a penalty shoot-out when John Aloisi scored the final penalty for a 4–2 victory. Australia performed well in the group stages in Germany, beating Japan 3–1 when Tim Cahill scored their first ever goal in a World Cup Finals. They then lost 0–2 to Brazil and drew 2–2 with Croatia. Australia made it into the knock-out stage, where they lost 0–1 to a dubious penalty scored by Francesco Totti of Italy, with what was virtually the last kick of the game. The Socceroos have qualified for the World Cup Finals on every occasion since, but their performance in Germany remains their most outstanding effort. The players from that squad are still known as "the golden generation".

2007 turned out to be a memorable year for all the players who'd played for Australia since their first international game in 1922 against New Zealand, for the Football Federation of Australia decided to award a cap to every living player who had represented Australia in international football. In my case, it was 42 years after the event, but it was nevertheless an unforgettable all-expenses-paid evening at the Returned & Services League (RSL) Club in Batemans Bay, New South Wales. I was presented with my cap as the 172nd player to represent Australia.

Interestingly, a few years after that, I read an article in the *Barnsley Chronicle* about a party of Australian under-16 footballers who were on tour in England and were staying at the Wentworth Castle Northern College in Barnsley. I visited the college and introduced myself to the coach, Geoff Stanmore, as an ex-Socceroo, striking up a friendship with him. Geoff is a teacher at Bossley Park High School in western Sydney, and is one of the top coaches, if not *the* top coach, of schoolboys in Australia. He's dedicated to the job and brings a squad of under-16 schoolboys to the UK every year, usually to the Nottingham area, which means that I get to see him regularly. Likewise, I also go to see him at his school when I'm in Australia, which helps me to keep in touch with the development of football down under. The evidence shows a vast improvement since the 1960s when I played there. I'm strongly of the belief that the first World Cup qualifier against North Korea in 1965, regardless of the score, was that "first step in a 1,000-mile journey", just as the Chinese philosopher, Lao Tzu, historically recorded between the 6th and 4th century BC.

In 2015, I returned from a trip to Graceland (the home of Elvis) in the USA to see that I had received an invitation from the Football Federation of Australia (FFA) to attend an official reunion on 16th November 2015 in Sydney.

Only 14 out of the original 20 in the 1965 squad were able to attend the reunion. They were: John Roberts, Bill Rorke, Nigel Shepherd, Stan Ackerley, Pat Hughes, Les Scheinflug, Geoff Sleight, John Anderson, Archie Blue, John Watkiss, Dave Todd,

156

Roy Blitz, Jimmy Pearson and Ron Giles. Sadly, Bill Rice, Billy Cook, Hammy McMeechan, Steve Herczeg, Ian Johnston and Johnny Warren missed it because of illness or having passed away. Unfortunately, John Anderson passed away in July 2021, while I was writing this book.

At the event, David Gallop, the FFA chief executive, paid tribute to our 1965 squad. He said, "These pioneers laid the foundations of the future World Cup qualifying campaigns and broke new ground under trying conditions and with extremely limited resources as they travelled to play in a place totally foreign to them. Considering the challenges they faced, and the magnitude of what they were up against, these trailblazers epitomise what it means to represent your country. They have, and will continue to leave, a lasting legacy for Australian football."

David Gallop then presented us with a replica football shirt sporting the number 65 to represent the year of our involvement, and medals indicating that we were pioneers in the development of football in Australia. The reunion then progressed from the presentation at the FFA headquarters in the city to Homebush, the home of the Olympic Stadium, which had been renamed ANZ Stadium. There, the 1965 players doubled up with those who had beaten Uruguay in 2005 and were now celebrating the 10th anniversary of that momentous victory. A gala dinner was held at the stadium, hosted by Frank Lowy, the retiring chairman of the FFA and the multi-billionaire owner of the global Westfield Shopping Centre group.

Since 2016, my involvement in football has been limited to regular contact and discussions on the telephone or internet with football historians in Australia. These include Roy Hay, Greg Stock, Doug Butcher and George Cotsanis. It's heartening that they, mainly Roy Hay, are continually researching football in the country, going way back in time to the Aboriginal people playing football, or a version of it, long before the first international game in 1922. It seems that the professional game developed rapidly when Australian clubs increased the number of players being signed from Europe and South America in the late 1950s and early 1960s. As this included my era, the historians seem particularly interested in my opinion relating to the mid-1960s. I'm flattered by their interest, and more than happy that they seem to value what I have to say. At the same time, they are keeping me in touch with what's happening down under, which doesn't seem to interest the media in the UK as much as it ought to, particularly considering the number of Australian players in Europe as a whole.

Figure 42 With Dave Todd at Everton to meet the North Koreans in October 2002.

Figure 43 On the pitch at Everton with the North Korean players and Dave Todd. I am wearing my red jacket.

Figure 44 Surviving members of the 1965 North Korean team at Everton in October 2002.

Figure 45 Rim Jong Son with his family in Pyongyang, 2002.

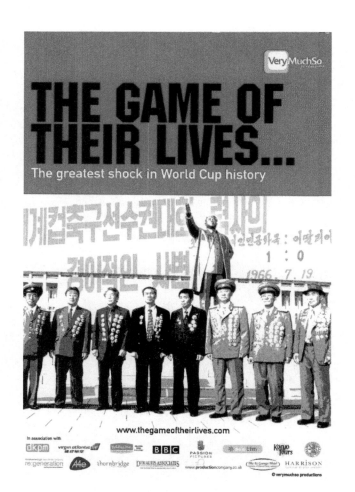

Figure 46 Front cover of the book, "The Game of Their Lives" with the North Koreans.

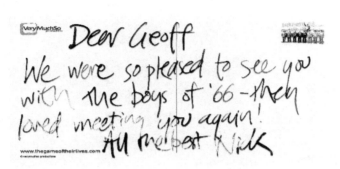

Figure 47 Appreciation from Nick at VeryMuchSo productions, who made the film "The Game of Their Lives."

Figure 48 Socceroos cap Presentation in Batemans Bay, New South Wales, 2007.

Figure 49 Checking on the Ashes score in England at the cap presentation 2007.

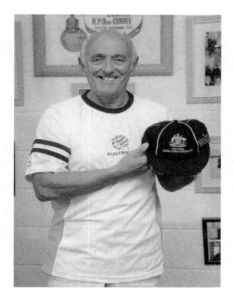

Figure 50 Socceroos cap from 1965 presented in 2007.

Figure 51 If the cap fits, wear it!

Figure 52 World Cup cap 172, presented in 2007. Medal presented by King Norodom Sihanuck in 1965."Pioneers" medal presented by the FFA in 2015.

Figure 53 Presentation of the "Pioneers Medal" by David Gallop, Chief Executive at the FFA in 2015.

Figure 54 Presentation of the commemorative shirts for the 1965 World Cup squad.

Figure 55 With Dave Todd in Sydney, 2015.

Figure 56 With Dave Todd at the 50-year reunion dinner in Sydney, 2015.

Figure 57 Photograph with Dave Todd, Ron Lord and Jimmy Pearson at the 50-year Socceroos reunion, 1965.

Figure 58 Peggy and myself all dressed up for the Gala Dinner in 2015.

Figure 59 At Canape's having a snack with Sofia Angelakis and Nick Duke, friends from the FFA.

Figure 60 Being interviewed by Glen Lauder in 2015 for a presentation on Fox Sports TV.

168

Figure 61 Talking to football students at Bossley Park High School with coach Geoff Stanmore in 2015.

Figure 62 At Bossley High School with coaches Geoff Stanmore and Neil Mann and two aspiring Socceroos, Fabian Monge and Thomas Aquilina.

CHAPTER NINE

How Football Has Changed

I think the increase in coaching is the major change in football since I was a youngster. Back then, we would have a bit of shooting practice and a bit of heading practice. Now, it's all moved on so much. We used to play on Good Friday, Easter Saturday and Easter Monday; three times in four days. It was the same at Christmas – we played on Christmas Day and Boxing Day. Nowadays, I think there's a lot more care taken with the health of players – they won't overtrain them and more attention is given to diet. When we used to do pre-season training, there weren't many exercises except a few sit-ups – it was all run, run, run. Run until you drop. You don't get that nowadays; it's all measured and timed.

When I started playing, there were no substitutes allowed. If you were travelling to a game, you'd take 12 men on the bus, but only in case one got sick on the way! In 1961, Leeds United were playing at Southampton and the goalkeeper either got sick or was injured. They'd taken 12 players down there, but the 12th man wasn't a goalkeeper. So, they flew Gary Sprake down by helicopter and he made his debut against Southampton at just 16 years old!

I'm sure that there are now a lot of youngsters who are spotted at seven years old and then, by the time they're nine, it's decided that they should be released. That didn't happen in my day. My own personal opinion is that nine is too young to make a decision about a player's future potential, but I put it down to the level of greed and competitiveness that we now have in football. When I was seven years old, I might have been 2ft 1in and one stone two – nobody knew whether or not I was going to grow. As it turned out, I didn't grow much, but a lot of kids go on to grow much bigger – some even get too big to play football. There was no forward planning when I was playing for my junior school and around the council estate, and now I think there's too much forward planning.

Another major change is the dominance of agents and money within the game, and that is something which I think can be linked to the Bosman ruling in 1995. When I went to play in Australia, I had to have clearance from my existing club – I had to be released by Wigan before I could play for Prague. In those days, if a player signed a contract for a year, that meant that after 12 months, he would either be retained or released. If he was retained then he couldn't leave, and there was no time limit on how long a club could retain you – they could do it year after year if they wanted to. That all changed when a player called Jean-Marc Bosman went to court in Europe to challenge the validity of retained contracts. Now, if you sign a contract for three years, when those three years have elapsed, you're free to go. Take, for example, Harry Kane, who's

171

currently worth something in the region of £150 million. He's out of contract at the end of the 2024 season, and if he wants to leave Spurs at that point, the club will get nothing for him. If, however, they convince him to sign a new contract, then he'll have to stay with them for the duration of that contract, unless the club agree to release him early – i.e., if another club comes and offers Spurs such a huge amount of money for him that they'll accept it.

This freedom of contract rule gave rise to an aspect of football which I don't like, but which is now as much a part of the game as kicking the ball – agents. Agents came into being as a major force in the game from 1995 onwards. In my opinion, agents and inflation are the reasons that players' incomes have risen to their current phenomenal levels. I feel that the agents focus too much on money. To me, everything is now based on one question: "How much money can we get?"

When I worked at Leeds in the mid-1990s, the top-paid players were on £6,000 per week. At the time of writing, the top-paid players like Messi and Ronaldo are on over £1 million per week. Players, through their agents, can ask for whatever wages they want, on the basis that if they don't get them, they can walk away to another club willing to meet their pay demand. This is essentially allowing players to hold their clubs to ransom. One of my friends once told me, "I can't believe you're not an agent."

I replied, "I can't believe I'm not an agent, except it's not honest enough for me."

As I've said repeatedly in this book, I've never grown beyond 5ft 4in. Being small, I found myself being played as a winger, and in later years (when I played non-league) I played in any position, including midfield and even full-back sometimes. I headed the ball more than most little guys, but I'm now glad that I wasn't a big guy because I wouldn't have wanted to head the ball all the time. In those days, you didn't head the ball, the heavy ball headed you! As we're all getting older, many of those players who headed the ball a lot seem to be developing dementia. Having said that, even I sometimes find myself going upstairs only to realise I've forgotten what I went up for! However, I can still remember goals I scored as a schoolboy in exact detail.

In an interview for a publication on the internet called *Walking Down the Manny Road*, I was asked who had influenced me the most in my football life. My reply was that nobody had enough of an influence on me to save a career that promised so much but delivered so little. However, I said, I had no regrets. The fault was mine and nobody else's. I would say that if you had a scale of all the people who ever played football, with local footballers at the bottom and people like Pelé, Maradona and George Best at the top, in my early years I would've been in the top 1%. I did have success, playing for

173

England schoolboys and the Australian international team, but I didn't achieve all that I feel I might've been capable of. There are certain parts of my personality which have either held me back or driven me. I think most of them have driven me. The word "feisty" has followed me my entire career. I don't kid myself about it; I know myself and it's true. It's my personality and I can't change it.

I was also asked if I had any regrets. My answer was that I don't. I don't do regrets because you can't change anything that's in the past.

CHAPTER TEN

Famous Faces

Alan Ball

Around 1983, I had nothing to do with football. Instead, I was big into horseracing. One day, I was at Salisbury Races with my son, Jeremy, when we saw Alan Ball walking towards us. Jeremy wanted to get Alan's autograph and so approached him to ask for it. Alan hadn't seen me and, as he was signing for my son, I walked up and said, "Well, Bally, it's a long time since I signed one of those."

Alan remarked, "Geoff! How are you doing?"

Jeremy looked agog, and asked me, "Dad, do you *know* him? You never told me you knew him!"

We all had a chat and then went our separate ways. We hadn't gone ten yards before I saw Jenny Pitman standing there. She had just won the Grand National that year with Corbiere. A friend of mine from Royston, Bryan Smart, is a racehorse trainer and he used to ride for Jenny. I said to Jeremy, "Why don't you go and ask for that lady's autograph?"

Jenny Pitman was, and is, the most famous woman trainer in horseracing history and Jeremy asked, "Who's she?" Jenny just laughed and signed her autograph.

Interestingly, as I was writing this book, I saw that the autograph of Sir Stanley Matthews was sold for £130 on the TV programme *Dickinson's Real Deal*, where people sell such memorabilia. This raises the question of the value of some of the autographs I have in my possession. As well as Jeremy having Alan Ball's and Jenny Pitman's, I have a Manchester United programme signed by Sir Matt Busby on 6th February 1993, the 35th anniversary of the Munich air crash, and the autograph of Sir Stanley Matthews on one of my "Leeds United Chief Scout" business cards. Any buyers?

When I was chief scout at Leeds United in 1996, I went to Bolton to watch a match. They put my wife and I in the directors' box in the main stand. All of a sudden, there was a bit of a problem – a lot of noise and swearing going on. The directors' box wasn't that far above the terrace so we could hear all the comments and swearing. Some of the Bolton supporters had seen Alan Ball, and they were really having a go at him. His wife took her high-heeled shoe off and was smashing the supporters with it, telling them to leave him alone! Bally was just sitting there while his wife defended him! He couldn't have leaned over himself or they would've grabbed him, so she did it for him.

Chris Kamara

While I was working at Leeds United, Alan Ball was the

manager of Stoke City. One of his players was Chris Kamara, who I'd watched play two or three times. My role working for Howard Wilkinson wasn't just watching games and doing match reporting, it was doing everything, and one of my jobs was chatting to players we might be about to sign. This particular day, Chris Kamara was at Leeds, sitting and chatting with me, and I had the television on in the corner of the office. Alan Ball popped up on it. He was being interviewed and was asked if Kamara was about to be sold. He said he didn't know. Alan was then asked where Kamara was at the moment, and he replied that he didn't know because he hadn't seen him for two days. I was shouting at the television, "Bally, he's here with me!"

I think we signed Kamara about two days later. He was a good player and I got to know him quite well. Stoke were in a lower division at the time, and Chris did everything while he played with them: he took the throw-ins, he took the free kicks, and he wasn't bad at giving people a kick! Knowing his personality, you wouldn't think that he was like that on the football pitch. He was always grateful that Howard gave him his chance to play in the top league. Leeds kept him for a season and then sold him to Sheffield United, but Leeds was the highest peak in his career. He's since gone on to television as a presenter and pundit and I have to say, I think he's brilliant.

Francis Lee

In 1971, I went to see my pal Francis Lee at home one day. Francis became a great friend of mine when we were kids together at Bolton, and in his career he played 27 times for England, including in the 1970 World Cup. Apparently, he was the first Englishman to be booked in a World Cup game, when England played Brazil.

In the early 1970s, I was driving a Mini – registration number GHL785D. The letters HL represented the vehicle registration centre at Wakefield. Francis's full name is Francis Henry Lee and he knew that I had some friends who worked in the vehicle registration centre. He asked if I could make some enquiries with them about getting him the registration number FHL1, FHL10 (10 was his number at Manchester City) or FHL7 (7 was his number for England). I made some enquiries and they turned up FHL7. It was owned by some guy who lived way up in the Pennines. I drove up there in late November and knocked on the door. I introduced myself and asked if he had the vehicle FHL7. He said that it was a BSA 125 Bantam motorbike, but had since been scrapped. However, he still had the logbook which gave you ownership of the registration number. I offered him £15 for the book, but he said he wanted £25. I came home and rang Francis to tell him what I'd found out. Francis said, "Offer him £20 and give him £25 if you have to." I went back up to the top of the Pennines the next evening and ended up giving the guy £25 for the logbook.

Shortly after that, Francis was due to play for England against Switzerland, and I told him I wanted two tickets for the game in return for bringing the logbook down to him at the hotel in Hertfordshire. I went down there and gave him the book, and got my two tickets for the game in return. At that point, Alan Ball walked in and said, "Geoff, can you get me AB1?" I said I would try, but I knew he had no chance!

Francis put his FHL7 number on a Bentley and then on a Rolls Royce. Then, he thought maybe the Rolls Royce was a bit too showy, so he went back to the Bentley. At the time, the most expensive car registration number in England cost £250,000 and it was ELV1S – my hero. The comedian Jimmy Tarbuck had COM1C, and the DJ Tony Blackburn had RAD1O1. People are still paying a lot of money for number plates like those, and they're only going up in value because you can't create new ones anymore. I was offered £500 for mine just the other month, which is C6CKJ. I bought a Mercedes about 20 years ago from a guy whose initials were KJ. He owned his own company, and whenever anyone asked a question in the company, they would be told, "See KJ," so the registration number was a reference to that. I think most personalised number plates tend to be related to the ego of the individual.

During my years in horseracing, Francis Lee once phoned me up and told me that he had a box at the upcoming charity weekend of racing at York. He told me, "Bring your football boots with you."

"Why?" I asked.

"I'll tell you when you get here."

We duly arrived and Francis said, "No drinking, no Veuve Clicquot, because after the racing, we're playing a charity football match in the middle of the racetrack against Jim McGrath's team." Jim McGrath was a racing pundit who worked for Timeform. He also played in a football team called Timeform, which had won the Halifax League. The previous year, they'd held a similar match and Francis had turned up with all these old newspaper writers and racing correspondents in his team. They had been well beaten! All McGrath did for the next 12 months was tease and torment Francis about it. Francis was now fed up with it, so this year, he had a goalkeeper from Rochdale, Colin Bell (ex-Manchester City and England) at centre-half, me in midfield, and Francis himself up front. The rest were newspaper men, but we didn't need them. We beat McGrath's team 4–2 and I remember Francis saying, "That'll shut him up!" Jim McGrath was a nice guy, but he was as upset at having been beaten as Francis had been the previous year. Whenever I saw Jim at future races, he would always grumble about how Francis had brought me and the others in to beat him.

On another occasion, Francis had two runners at York and three runners at Towcester on the same day. As often happened in these circumstances, Francis asked if I wanted to go to Towcester as his representative. Obviously, I jumped at the opportunity and went with Peggy to have an interesting day out. Shortly before the first race at 2pm, in which Sagareme, the first of Francis's three runners, was running, Peggy went to the ladies' room. When she came back, she said that I would never guess who she'd been talking to while she was there. She was right; I would indeed never have guessed that she'd met Princess Anne, who happened to be riding in the first race. There were no ladies' changing facilities in those days, so HRH had to change in the ladies' toilets. Shortly afterwards, Sagareme won the first race. It was a "selling plate race", which meant that the winner was available for purchase by the highest bidder during an auction held immediately after the race. I called Francis at York and asked him if he wanted to "buy the horse in". In the conditions of a selling plate race, a horse could be retained by the owner providing he made the highest bid. He told me to go up to 2,000 guineas or let the horse go to a higher bidder (one guinea was the value of £1.05).

I attended the auction and explained to the auctioneer that as Mr Lee's representative, I would be bidding for the horse, and would be easily recognised by the bright yellow jacket I was wearing that day. Bidding began at 800 guineas. The auctioneer then looked at me; I nodded my head and the price went up to 1,000 guineas. There was a bid of 1,100 guineas, after which Peggy said, "Geoff, stop nodding your head. Every time you do, the price goes up by 100 guineas." She didn't realise that I was bidding on up to 2,000 guineas to keep the horse on Francis's behalf and would let it go only if the bid went higher than 2,000. In the end, the horse was "bought in" because my bid of 1,700 guineas was the highest. I agreed the purchase with the auctioneer and told him to charge the 1,700 guineas to Francis Lee's account at Weatherbys (who deal with horseracing finances). The auctioneer explained that this could not be done; the payment of the horse had to be made in cash before it could be allowed to leave the racecourse. I called Francis at York and explained the situation to him. He told me to tell the auctioneer to charge the cost to Weatherbys. When I told Francis that this wasn't allowed, his reaction was, "Sleighty, you are the owner, you are there, you sort it out."

How was I going to find 1,700 guineas? As it happened, the prize money of about 850 guineas was taken into consideration. One of the other two runners then finished third in a later race, securing prize money of 350 guineas. Peggy had 150 guineas and I had backed a couple of winners, which added another 250 guineas to the total. Steve Holland, the jockey, had 100 guineas or so in his pocket, giving us just enough to allow the horse to be released, with £10 left just in case we needed some petrol on the way home!

Being a racehorse owner is not necessarily as glamourous as it appears to be!

Francis is now a multi-millionaire, through his business acumen. It's odd that we get on, since he doesn't like Yorkshiremen. He once told me that he wouldn't have signed for Leeds United even if they'd offered him £1 million. I reminded him that I was from Yorkshire and he said, "Ah, but you don't count!"

Mick Morgan

I was invited to a men-only charity evening at Castleford Rugby League Club, hosted by former Great Britain rugby league player Mick Morgan. I didn't realise at the time that he'd been in the first year at Normanton Grammar School when I was in the sixth year. Guests included several other noted rugby league players, many Castleford players, and several ex-professional footballers.

Before he began his hilariously funny after-dinner speech, Mick introduced the sporting personalities to the audience. Mick made a particular joke of the four or five footballers, the most well-known of which was Rod Belfitt, who had played for Leeds United, Ipswich Town, Everton, Sunderland and Huddersfield. He introduced the last football player by saying, "Finally, the best player I have ever seen or remember is Geoff Sleight, who played at Normanton Grammar School when I was there." That is the most impromptu compliment that I've ever received.

By sheer coincidence, within a year, my wife and I met Mick Morgan and his wife Brenda on a cruise from Hong Kong to Sydney. For the next two or three weeks, we never stopped laughing from beginning to end – cheers Mick!

Other Big Names

There are so many well-known people and places in football today that I seem to have a connection to. I'll regularly be watching the TV and see a ground that I've been to or someone I played against years ago. I just seem to have a finger in every pie in football.

Denis Law had his peak at Manchester United. He won the Ballon d'Or while playing for them in 1965. By 1974, his career was winding down, and he'd returned to Manchester City. On 27th April, Denis was playing for City against United. From a pass by Francis Lee, Denis backheeled the ball into the Manchester United goal, causing the relegation of his former club.

That same night, Francis Lee had his birthday party and we had a few whiskies. Denis Law was there, and he was really fed up because he had relegated Manchester United. "It's my job," he said miserably. "I had to do it." Denis had played with Huddersfield, then Manchester City, then Torino, and had then spent 11 years at Manchester United. He was one of the all time greats of the game.

I met a lot of famous players, but I never met George Best or Bobby Charlton. I played at least four or five times for Manchester All-Stars, which Francis Lee used to help run. Whenever Bobby Charlton wasn't available, I would play instead, which meant that we never met. On 7th October 1979, we played Liverpool All-Stars at Chorley. What a game that was! We kicked lumps off each other. I wish I could remember everyone who was in their team. I know that Keith Newton from Burnley and England played at left-back; Tommy Wright from Everton played right-back; Roger Hunt of Liverpool and England played; as did Roy Evans, who later became Liverpool manager. Roy Evans did me right on my stocking top! I was only 36 then, so I was still nippy. I still owe you one Roy, and Yorkshiremen are like elephants – they never forget...

LEEDS UNITED F.C.
Elland Road
Leeds LS11 OES
'Phone 0532 716037

With the Compliments of

G. SLEIGHT
Representative
LEEDS UNITED F.C.

5 The Courtyard
Woolley
Wakefield WF4 2LY   'Phone 0226-385627 (H)

Figure 63 Leeds United business card, 1994-96.

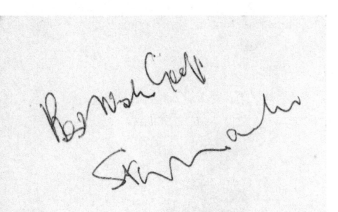

Figure 64 Sir Stanley Matthews' autograph on the back of a Leeds United business card, 1994.

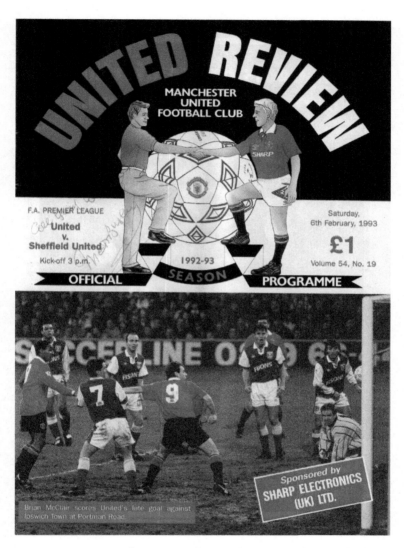

Figure 65 Front cover of programme for Manchester United versus Sheffield United, autographed by Sir Matt Busby on 6th February 1993.

187

Figure 66 Inkosi, winner of the Barclays Bank Handicap, at Thirsk. With me, Francis Lee and the stable lad, 3rd August 1991.

Figure 67 My younger son Jeremy, my wife Peggy, Trevor Lee and winner Miramac at Keslo in October 1985.

Figure 68 Horse racing with Francis Lee, another winner.

Figure 69 Mick Morgan and me in Brunei on a cruise from Hong Kong to Sydney.

Figure 70 Mick Morgan and me with Dnani Moorcroft, a singer and dancer on the Oriana cruise ship, 2012.

CHAPTER ELEVEN

Other Sports

Horseracing

I have written to a greater or lesser degree about football, Australia and horseracing, so it would be remiss of me if I didn't mention the horse that links together Australia and horseracing. This horse is Black Caviar, a filly and later a mare who was unbeaten in 25 races over 4 years, and who travelled from Melbourne to Royal Ascot in 2012 to win the Diamond Jubilee Stakes, a Group One six-furlong race. On the 30-hour flight from Australia to the UK, the horse wore a compression suit to help blood circulation throughout the journey. Racing over a straight six furlongs on rain-softened ground, Black Caviar won by a head from the French-trained filly, Moonlight Cloud, a multi-Group One winner in Europe. The jockey, Luke Nolen, sent the mare to the front inside the last two furlongs, but after establishing a clear lead began to ease Black Caviar. Moonlight Cloud moved up on the stand side to draw almost level before Nolen began driving Black Caviar again in the final strides. Nolen said that his overconfidence had been a factor in the closeness of the finish. It was discovered during X-rays after the race that Black Caviar had sustained an 8cm muscle tear at some point during the race. Nolen felt the change in the horse and said that he thought she'd done enough to get home. Peter Moody, the trainer, explained that the mare hadn't coped with the 11,000-mile journey as well as he'd hoped or expected. An examination by veterinarian Peter Angus and chiropractor Michael Bryan later revealed that Black Caviar sustained a Grade Four tear of the quadriceps and a Grade Two tear of the sacroiliac during the race. Black Caviar returned to Australia and recovered, going on to be unbeaten in 25 races, including 15 Group One races, breaking the Australian record for Group One wins. A true champion by any standards. I was so thrilled and impressed with Black Caviar's performance that I wrote to the trainer's secretary, Marni Kelly, the partner of Tony Haydon, who actually looked after the horse. I'm still in regular contact with Marni and Tony, who have their own racing stables up on the sunshine coast in Queensland. They're hoping for another Black Caviar!

Rugby Union

Having successfully negotiated and survived the one game of rugby league that I played when I was in Australia, I had a similar experience when I was working at the West Riding Education Department in Wakefield. The local authority staff traditionally played rugby union against the West Riding Constabulary on a home and away basis every couple of years. In the late 1960s, Brian Appleton, a friend and colleague in the same office as me, played in the home game. When he told me the following day that they had lost the game 67–0, it upset him that I laughed at the score! Brian got annoyed and retaliated by telling me that I was a "soft soccer player" and wouldn't even be able to last a game of rugby union, regardless of how they'd played in their game against the police.

As usual, it was like a red rag to a bull, and I suggested that he arrange for me to play in the return away game at Knottingley the following week. It transpired that the stand-off half was injured, and I was asked if I would like to put my money where my mouth was and play in his place. I played, we won the game 12–9, and I scored a winning penalty try! This happened after I was through for a certain touchdown – I was winning the race towards a loose ball, from which I would've scored a try, when I was flattened off the ball. The try was converted and we won the game, which means that my rugby union career is almost identical to my rugby league career: played one, won one, scored one try. Not exactly Johnny Wilkinson, but a 100% record nonetheless.

Golf

I played a bit of golf during the 1970s, but never threatened to become an Arnold Palmer or a Gary Player (two of the world's all time greats). I have lived in Woolley village since 1982, and in 1995 the Rowbottom family, who own a great deal of land in the village, developed and opened what is now called Woolley Park Golf Club just half a mile down the road. I couldn't resist the temptation and became a full member that same year. I began to play regularly, particularly after I had finished working for Leeds United at the end of 1996. I was never technically gifted as a golf player, but I was competitive enough to achieve scores that got my handicap down as low as 10. During the course of this time, I became the first member to win all three of the club's senior competitions: the Crossley Plate, the Seniors Cup and the Goodrich Cup (which was basically the Seniors' Championship).

After I had both my hips replaced in 2007, playing golf was a big challenge and I was not as effective as I had been, particularly in terms of winning. I never actually enjoyed playing golf for the sake of it, but I loved the competitiveness and the prospect of winning. When I had both my hips replaced again in 2013, I was no longer able to win and lost my enjoyment of golf, and because I didn't fancy playing the game just for the sake of playing, I gave it up. I don't miss playing golf, but I do miss the opportunity of playing to win. More to the point, I miss actually winning. My only involvement with the golf club nowadays is to take visitors there for lunch or to call in for a drink with my friends Carol and Roger Wood on Saturday afternoons.

Nevertheless, there were three special occasions in my golfing career that remain memorable.

Firstly, I got a hole-in-one on the par three ninth hole. Unfortunately, the downside of this achievement is that I'd gone to the golf club one sunny afternoon to play nine holes by myself to pass a couple of hours, so I have no witnesses to my once-in-a-lifetime special golf shot. The upside is that I didn't have to buy the customary bottle of whisky in the bar for members to toast my magical shot.

Secondly, on 11th November 2011, i.e. 11/11/11, Derek Farrar, one of our regular four-ball, scored a hole-in-one at the 11th hole at 11 minutes to 11. The odds of that happening are infinitesimal. I thought that the golf club should call *Calendar* at Yorkshire TV and get a reporter down to the club to interview Derek. However, Derek didn't even go back into the clubhouse. I suspect that he didn't want to provide the necessary bottle of whisky for members to drink to his great achievement!

Thirdly, our regular four-ball of Derek Farrar, Keith Simpson, myself and Jim Hirst played off handicaps of 23, 10, 10 and 8 respectively. One day, we all birdied the 571-yard par five eighth hole in the same round. Though not the same lengthy odds as Derek's hole-in-one, the odds were nevertheless long enough to win a lot of money if you had a £1 bet on it.

Cricket

If my ability to play football at the highest level was born and nurtured during my early years living on a council estate in Royston, then so was my ability to play cricket. I played in my junior school team at the age of 10 and 11 as a batsman and bowler, and in later years as a high order batsman and wicketkeeper. I played for Royston Cricket Club in the second 11 from the age of 12, progressing to the first 11 from the age of 16 onwards. At the same time, I progressed through my years at Normanton Grammar School playing in the under-14s, and then played for the first 11 from the age of 14.

My first game for the first 11 at Normanton Grammar School at the age of 14 was probably the highlight of my cricket life. I played against Hemsworth Grammar School, who batted first, their opening batsman being a lad named Geoffrey Boycott. Now Sir Geoffrey, he went on to be opening batsman for both Yorkshire and England, scoring 100 centuries during his career. When we were rained off at 142 for 4, Boycott was 107 not out. In his book he says he was 105 not out, but I remember it differently. I did play against him again some years later in a senior knock-out competition at Shaw Lane in Barnsley. My friend, Keith Wilson, got Boycott out for nine and we did win that game.

Boycott was a very good batsman, but he did practise the philosophy that can be summed up as, "Don't be out". That sounds simple, but as a result of it, Boycott had some incredibly long innings. He also had no qualms about running out his batting partner rather than being run out himself. That, amongst other things, made him a controversial person, but nevertheless, "Don't be out" is still the advice I give my grandsons Reuben and George, who both play cricket.

Until comparatively recently, Boycott lived just across the road from me. People have always had a lot to say about him. Some people love him to pieces and some don't like him at all. His personality doesn't promote friendliness, so what I'm about to say is not said under the guise of his being a friend of mine – it's just my opinion, and we're all entitled to one of those.

Some years ago, Geoffrey Boycott was with a lady friend in France. They had an argument and she claimed that he hit her, which Boycott denied. It came to court in France and Boycott produced six female witnesses to testify about his personality. Apparently, the woman wanted to marry him and, when he refused, she got annoyed and, allegedly, attacked him. It seems that the judge in France didn't believe Boycott, and he was found guilty of assault.

A few years later, I was on the beach in Barbados. Two locals heard me speak and said that I sounded like Boycott. They told me they didn't like Boycott, and when I asked why not, they replied, "He beat women." I told them that I didn't think he was guilty and that, in my opinion, the verdict was wrong. The

West Indian guys began calling to their friends to tell them that I knew Boycott and said that he was innocent. Ten seconds later, I had eight Bajan guys listening to my story! They believed me, and later admitted that they liked Boycott again as a result. A couple of years ago, I met Boycott's solicitor and told them that Geoffrey owes me a pint! Whether I ever get it or not is another matter. Regardless, Geoffrey Boycott was a great cricketer, and that's what he'll be remembered for.

Back to my own cricketing career. In 1955, I played for the second team at Royston in an away match against a team called Stanley in the West Riding League. During the match, I took such a good catch that the players had a collection for me and raised £1! The money enabled me to go to Headingly the following Monday to watch England play South Africa in the fourth test match in their series. While playing for the first team a few years later, just before my 18th birthday, I scored 94 not out in a partnership of 144 with my school pal Keith Wilson. As a reward, I was presented with a Len Hutton Slazenger cricket bat at the end of the season. The presentation was made by Dorothy Hyman, the local sprinter and double medallist in the 1960 Olympic Games.

After reaching the final of the West Riding League Cup in 1967 and 1968, we went on to win the West Riding League Division One and were promoted to the Pontefract section of the Yorkshire Council. The team were performing reasonably well in the higher league, but in July, I had a bit of a spat with the captain, Malcolm Holling, who was a good friend of mine. The season was clashing with friendly football matches during Buxton's pre-season preparation for the forthcoming football season. I left Royston Cricket Club and played the next three games for the West Riding County Council NALGO team (National Association of Local Government Officers), before football took over. I scored 55, 54 and 25 in those games, playing against Altofts, Whitley Bridge and Featherstone respectively. Those clubs held the top three positions in the league at the time. Added to my scores at Royston, I finished with a season average of 50.5 runs, which would've been third in the whole of the Yorkshire Council. Unfortunately, Royston would not submit the runs that I'd scored for them, so the Yorkshire Council wouldn't recognise my overall average for the season.

I then basically retired from competitive cricket, but I did play for the Barnsley Council team in the NALGO Cup in 1974. I scored 105 not out against Huddersfield and we went on to win the cup against Humberside. The following season, we lost in the final to Wakefield Council at Castleford.

From then on, I played little cricket until 1983, when Derek Powers, a lifetime friend of mine, took over Royston Cricket Club. I had played for them previously, and halfway through the season, he asked me to play for the club again. I didn't have any involvement in football at the time, so I agreed to help him out. Without doing anything exceptional, I topped the batting average. For some reason that I don't recall, I didn't go to the celebratory dinner. It wasn't until six or seven years ago that there was a knock at the front door. Apparently, the club had been having a clear out and found the trophy that I was supposed to have received. It was presented to me on the doorstep over 30 years late!

My cricket standard was not as high as that which I reached playing football, but it was high enough to be proud of and a target in performance for the future generations.

Tennis

I played some tennis, but only really during the summer (around Wimbledon time) in the park with friends. I only ever played tennis competitively on one occasion, which was when Normanton Grammar School played against the Girls' High School on their court. I won the first set and was leading in the second set when we were rained off.

On one particularly funny occasion, during the Miners' Strike, Peggy and I took my sons Paul and Jeremy to Newquay on holiday, along with Jeremy's schoolfriend, Rob Landon. We were staying in a nice hotel which had tennis courts, and Rob and Jeremy wanted to play. The two boys formed a doubles partnership and Peggy and Paul agreed to be their opponents, while I sat on the high umpire seat. Rob used to get his words mixed up and he wasn't as competitive as Jeremy, so when Rob hit a bad shot and Jeremy started giving him a hard time about it, he got flustered and announced, "I've torn my armstring (*sic*)!" He'd got the word mixed up with his hamstring.

Squash

Squash was a comparatively new game in the 1960s. It came to prominence when a British player called Jonah Barrington became one of the top three players in the world, and as a result, the game took off. When I saw the game being played, it appealed to me because it seemed more active and aggressive than tennis.

I gave squash a try in the mid-1970s and I did OK. Because of my involvement in other sports, I never aimed to be at the top of the game, but I used it as a good way of keeping fit. You have to be as fit as anyone else alive to be any good at squash. If I played with friends or other people for whom squash wasn't their best sport, I could beat them, but whenever I came across dedicated squash players who represented clubs, they would beat me (although not without me giving them a good game). I would never claim to be as good at squash as I was at other sports, but

I was better than the average person.

Athletics

I was always sporty, but I was never an athlete *per se* when competing against the best in my school or in adult life. I was always better than average at sprinting and at longer distances, but the true athletes would always beat me. For example, in the 100-yard sprint at Normanton Grammar School on sports day, I ran the distance in 10.7 seconds and finished second. My house also won the relay race that day. I represented the school on two occasions in the 100-yard sprint at inter-school competitions, unfortunately finishing last of four and last of six respectively. I was quick, and certainly quick enough to get a place in the school team, but not quick enough to win. In my defence, Usain Bolt's not 5ft 4in! My legs could go as quick as his, but each stride was a yard shorter!

I was in the top six at cross-country in the school but was never good enough to win it. I finished 9th out of 16 when representing my school against Rishworth School in a three-mile race. In 1977, I finished halfway in a field of about 700 in the Barnsley six-mile road race. The first half a dozen finishers that day were international athletes. In 1983, I ran for Barnsley Council in the NALGO National Cross-Country Championships and finished around 150th out of 300. The positions are not very flattering on paper but on balance, I was a footballer and

202

cricketer and was running against proper athletes. If those finishing in front of me had competed against me in all my sports, then they would all presumably have finished behind me in terms of overall performance. Perhaps I should have been some sort of decathlete! I was a rounded performer in all aspects of football and cricket. I don't think for one minute that someone like Daley Thompson would have beaten me at football or cricket, or golf for that matter, but he's probably the best decathlete of all time in terms of running, jumping and throwing.

Athletic Feats for Children in Need

In later years, particularly 1989, 1991 and 1992, I was involved in raising money for the charity Children in Need. Although these occasions didn't involve football directly, they did call upon the athleticism which I had always relied upon to be effective in my life.

I was 46 years old in 1989 and had maintained a high level of fitness. That year, I agreed to do a triathlon involving a five-mile road run, a one-mile swim in a pool at one of the secondary schools, and a 25-mile bike ride. I suggested to my colleagues in the education department of Barnsley Council that I would do the deed if they would find sponsors for the Children in Need charity. They were all in favour of the arrangement. I set a four-hour time limit to complete the three distances, but actually aimed to do it in 2 hours 40 minutes. Sponsors would be asked to contribute a minimum of 1p per minute for every minute under the four-hours allowed.

I made good time in the five-mile run, but the one-mile swim nearly ended in disaster. After alternating between front crawl and breaststroke for about 10 minutes, hoping to complete the full distance in just over 30 minutes, I developed cramp in both my calves. This meant that I had to swim most of the remaining mile doing a very slow backstroke, which took over an hour. I then managed to complete the bike ride successfully in about 90 minutes. The time spent on the swim suggested that the money to be raised for the Children in Need appeal wouldn't be as much as we'd hoped.

In the event, thanks to the generous donations from the sponsors, the education department staff were able to raise over £1,000 for the 1989 appeal, with other departments also contributing similar amounts. In the late 1980s, £1,000 was worth considerably more than it is at the time of writing in 2021.

Two years later, in 1991, the education department staff wanted to make another effort for the Children in Need appeal and looked for ideas on how to do it. After consideration, I agreed to take a day of annual leave (as I had in 1989), during which I would stay in my office and aim to do a minimum of 1,000 press-ups, 1,000 exercises with the two 10kg weights, and 5,000 sit-ups. My time limit was the course of my normal working day: seven and a half hours, with an hour off for lunchbreak.

The disaster on this occasion had a much more beneficial outcome. Based on my intention to do a total of 7,000 exercises, it was suggested that sponsors pay 1p per 100 exercises: that is, 70p for the completion of the entire challenge. The "disaster" was that I actually completed 11,000 sit-ups, resulting in a total of 17,000 exercises, or £1.70 in sponsors' terms. At the end of it all, the staff raised £1,400 for the 1991 Children in Need appeal.

The Children in Need appeal came around again in the autumn of 1992, and after the success of the previous efforts, the staff wanted to do it again to raise more money for the charity. My contribution was that I agreed to dance non-stop in my office for the 24-hour period from 4pm on Thursday to 4pm on Friday, which was the actual day of the appeal. The decision on which music I would dance to was not a problem: it had to be Elvis. If there was no Elvis, there would be no dancing and no charity fundraising. The staff unanimously agreed to find sponsors. As a bonus, I also agreed that anybody within the department who wanted to come into my office to watch me dance would be charged 10p. To actually dance the jive or the twist with me would cost 50p. It all went very well from 4pm to 10pm on Thursday, as several of the staff came back into work for their Thursday evening out. The question of what would happen between 10pm and 8am the following morning was resolved when Peggy, my ever-loving wife, agreed to dance with me all through the night before she then went to work herself in Leeds. The night's session of dancing with Peggy was all smooching to songs such as *Love Me Tender, Loving You* and *I Can't Help Falling in Love with You*. It was an appropriate respite from *Hound Dog, Jailhouse Rock* and *Hard Headed Woman*! All day Friday, I moved into the director of education's office so that members of the whole department could call in for a dance at any time during the day. The staff raised £1,500 for the Children in Need appeal, which was a perfect example of the ends justifying the means.

Keeping Fit

I still maintain a high level of fitness at the time of writing, at the age of 78. I exercise regularly (seven days a week) in one form or another, be it walking, using the elliptical cross-trainer, cycling, or lifting two 10kg weights in my gym at home. Sometimes, I'm not sure whether this exercise is keeping me going or wearing me out! As I've mentioned, I've had both hips replaced twice – four hip replacements in total! However, most importantly, the indications are that my heart is strong.

Figure 71 In my gym with my football memorabilia.

Geoff's 'weighty' charity efforts

PRINCIPAL Administration Officer Geoff Sleight will spend today (Friday) exercising with weights — in aid of the BBC's Children in Need appeal.

Geoff, aged 48, who works with Barnsley Council's Education Department, aims to do a minimum of 1,000 exercises with weights, 5,000 sit-ups and 1,000 press-ups.

Former footballer Geoff, who represented Australia in the qualifying competition for the 1966 World Cup and played for Bolton Wanderers, has taken a day's holiday to do the fund-raising effort.

Geoff, of The Courtyard, Woolley said: "I exercise regularly to keep fit. I will make sure I rest regularly."

Geoff's effort is one of several fund-raising efforts being done today by Education Department staff.

Staff at Maplin's Electronics, Wombwell, have already collected £560 through fund-raising this week. Today worker David Haterall aims to add to that total by collecting around the factory dressed as a woman.

Trimetics Body Salon in King Street, Hoyland, is donating cash from customers who have body toning and back and neck massages today. Sisters Chris Mellor and Jayne Shaw, who run the salon, have organised face painting sessions for children.

Figure 72 Barnsley Chronicle report on Children in Need fundraising event in November 1991.

Plenty of fun and funds raised for Children in Need

BARNSLEY folk dug deep into their pockets to raise thousands of pounds for the Children in Need appeal last week.

Fund-raising fever gripped the town as Barnsley Council's Education Department raised a total of £1,400, mainly thanks to the efforts of Geoff Sleight who completed a marathon eight-hour session of press-ups and sit-ups.

Actor Stan Richards, better known as Emmerdale's Seth Armstrong, was also on hand to choose winning draw tickets and help out in other fund-raising events.

Meanwhile a sponsored shoe shine and a guess the value of the contents of a trolley competition gathered a total of £1,320 at Tescos, Stairfoot.

Staff at Mount Vernon Hospital donned fancy dress and collected £420, while Graham and Joanne Armitage of Lundwood Newsagents did the same, raising £211.

Children at Hunningley Lane Junior School used their free time to accumulate a proud total of £143 through events such as a face painting competition, disco and fancy dress.

Big-hearted staff at the Keresforth Children's Unit for the physically and mentally handicapped made and sold Pudsey Bear badges, raising £55.

PICTURED above: Lundw dealers Graham and Joann outfits raising money for Chi

BELOW: Staff at Mount Ver fancy dress outfits in a bid appeal. (BCP)

BELOW LEFT: Geoff Sleig Education Department rais was a marathon eight-hour se (BCP)

Figure 73 Barnsley Chronicle report on Children in Need fundraising event in November 1991.

Figure 74 Me lifting weights. Children in Need fundraiser,1991.

Figure 75 Photographs and memorabilia on my gym walls.

Figure 76 My 60th birthday cartoon.

Figure 77 Australian blazer and tracksuit top together with 1965 replica Socceroos shirt and shirts presented by Lucas Radebe and Philemon Masinga.

MISS DOROTHY HYMAN, Cudworth Olympic sprinter, presents a cricket bat to G. Sleight, adjudged the "most promising batsman," at the Royston Cricket Club dinner. Also in the picture, holding their trophies, are other prizewinners. (1600)

Figure 78 Presentation of a Len Hutton Slazenger cricket bat by Dorothy Hyman, a double medal winner in the Olympic Games in 1960.

212

CONCLUSION

People say I could talk for England, but I'm Australian now. At least, I am when it suits my purpose, such as when I'm watching the cricket! I'm proud to have played for Australia and to have my dual citizenship, but I'm also still a Yorkshireman – if I'm not happy about something, I'll tell you. I hope that saying things as I see them is one of my strengths. A Yorkshire Aussie – that's probably someone from Lancashire's worst nightmare!

Initially, the objective of this book was to recall and share my football memories. However, during the journey it has been both enlightening and interesting to remember all aspects of my sporting life, none of which have the depth of my football memories. It has been a gift that I could get involved in so many sporting activities during my life, all to a standard that allowed me to be competitive. It has educated me to realise that life is a series of challenges which encourage you to reach for the sky.

About the Author

Geoff Sleight was born on the 20th of June 1943. He was born in Royston, Yorkshire.

Apart from his love of football he has a great love for Elvis, who is one of his all time heroes alongside Serena Williams and Tiger Woods.

Geoff also had a passion and took great interest in horse racing. His favourite horse was Black Caviar. An Australian filly who came over to Royal Ascot and won the Diamond Jubilee Stakes. Black Caviar then went on to have 25 consecutive wins.

Geoff is proud of his dual citizenship but is always an Aussie where cricket is concerned!

He admires excellence and talent in all walks of life and is willing to give anyone a chance that he feels deserves one, this quality is what made him so successful in his sporting life off the field.

He is a very proud Dad and Grandad, one of the reasons he is writing this book is so his family can read all about his life and have a memory to cherish.

If you like the book and would love to pass on a message, you can reach Goeff via this email. yorkshireaussie@outlook.com

Printed in Great Britain
by Amazon

25403588R00119